Confronting Modernity

Joseph Federico

Confronting Modernity

Rationality, Science, and
Communication in German Literature
of the 1980s

CAMDEN HOUSE

First Edition

ISBN:1-879751-14-3

Printed by Thomson Shore, Inc.
Dexter, Michigan

Library of Congress Cataloging-in-Publication Data

Federico, Joseph, 1949-
    Confronting modernity : rationality, science, and communication in
German literature of the 1980s / Joseph Federico.
      p.   cm. -- (Studies in German literature, linguistics, and
culture ; v. 75)
    Includes bibliographical references and index.
    ISBN 1-879751-14-3 : $55.00
    1. German literature--20th century--History and criticism.
2. Science in literature. 3. Reason in literature.
4. Communication in literature.   I. Title. II. Series.
PT405.F43 1992
830.9'00914--dc20   92-6763
                                                                  CIP

Acknowledgments

I WOULD LIKE TO THANK Professors Beth Bjorklund (University of Virginia), Stephen Dowden (Yale University), and Jack Zipes (University of Minnesota) for reading the manuscript and offering valuable and much appreciated criticism.

I am also grateful to Dr. Michael Jordan, Acting Dean, University of St. Thomas, for his support.

Thanks are also due to Ms. Kristine Nitti, Department of Computing and Communication Services, University of St. Thomas, for patiently assisting me in the preparation of the manuscript and to Mr. Maurice Herzing for proofreading the final draft.

Portions of chapter 1 were previously published as part of "The Political Philosophy of Friedrich Dürrenmatt," *German Studies Review* 12 (1989): 91-109. Chapter 2 originally appeared as "Political Thinking in a Nuclear Age: Hochhuth's *Judith* and Dürrenmatt's *Achterloo*," *The German Quarterly* 62 (1989): 335-44. I am grateful to the editors of these journals for permission to reprint this material here.

For my parents

Human beings make everything paradoxical. Sense becomes nonsense; justice becomes injustice; freedom becomes bondage, because man is himself a paradox, an irrational rationality.

Friedrich Dürrenmatt, *Kants Hoffnung*

Contents

Preface

REPRESENTING THREE DIFFERENT COUNTRIES and forty years of literary production, the six writers discussed in this book would seem at first glance to have very little in common. What unites them, despite the diversity of style, outlook, and temperament their works exhibit, is an underlying preoccupation with rationality, specifically, with that mode of inquiry that traces its origins to the seventeenth century, that finds its ideal in science, and that has continued to dominate Western thought to the present day.

The central feature of this rational tradition has been the attempt to establish an "objective" method that would guarantee certainty. In recent years, this notion has been attacked by a number of thinkers, including Thomas Kuhn, Jürgen Habermas, Richard Rorty, and Paul Feyerabend, all of whom have rejected the notion that there can be a neutral, "objective" mode of inquiry or that there is any "rational" method that is unique to science. All methods of inquiry, it is claimed, are self-referential. There are no criteria that can guarantee certainty, objectivity, or truth. Thus, Richard Rorty has urged us to abandon the notion "that outside the haphazard and perilous experiments we perform there lies something (God, Science, Knowledge, Rationality, or Truth) which will, if only we perform the correct rituals, step in to save us."

In response to these developments, Rorty and Habermas have made what has come to be known as the "linguistic turn." Rather than reject reason outright, they invoke the other tradition of Western rationality, the one incorporated in the Socratic dialogue. This tradition has been exploited most thoroughly by Habermas, who claims that the locus of rationality is not the monologic, Cartesian subject but communicative action, which he describes as discourse oriented toward reaching understanding. In contrast to the technical rationality of science, which, Habermas claims, presents "the economy in the selection of purposive-rational means" as the sole admissible value, communicative reason is a comprehensive form of rationality that is rooted in the lifeworld. As linguistic beings, we are inextricably implicated in a "web of communicative action."

Discursive rationality is posited in every discourse oriented to consensus. Any individual entering into communicative action, Habermas maintains, raises validity claims to truth, rightness, and truthfulness, which can be redeemed through rational argument. In argumentation, the speaker must orient herself to an "ideal speech situation" characterized by reciprocity and an atmosphere free of constraints on dialogue. The norms posited by the ideal speech situation anticipate a dialogue society in which the truth can be freely pursued. Communicative reason is thus bound up with what Habermas calls the "project of modernity," whose goal is to foster emancipation by creating possibilities for communication free of domination. The success of this emancipatory project is dependent on the vitality of the public sphere, that admittedly idealized space, distinct from political institutions, where the public engages in uninhibited discourse. The "scientization of politics" and the manipulation of public opinion, Habermas claims, have led to the disintegration of the public sphere as the engine of free discourse and thus of social change.

The aim of this book is to investigate how this debate on rationality has played itself out in recent literature. Each of the authors discussed in the following chapters is responding in some way to the epistemic hegemony of science in modern society. Affirming science's preeminence, Friedrich Dürrenmatt and Rolf Hochhuth have attempted to incorporate scientific ideas constructively into their thinking. Strongly influenced by the epistemology of Sir Karl Popper, Dürrenmatt has even succeeded in reconciling scientific and communicative rationality. The other writers, by contrast, tend to equate scientific rationality with reason *tout court*. Overwhelmed by a technological society that proclaims instrumentality the highest value, they see little possibility for communicative action and the generation of new public meanings. As a response, their protagonists turn inward, seeking private meanings to replace public ones that are regarded as alien or unauthentic. This withdrawal, as a reaction to the disintegration of the public sphere, is perhaps their most pointed comment on the viability of the project of modernity.

Literature is, of course, by its nature a form of communication, and despite the skepticism toward communicative interaction that many of these works exhibit, they nevertheless contribute to public discussion (in the form of literary criticism) or at least to public awareness of these issues. Changing attitudes toward rationality, science, and communication — the three themes that resonate throughout this book — coincide with a generational shift in postwar German literature. As Stuart Parkes has recently observed in his introduction to *Literature on the Threshold: The German Novel in the 1980s*, the first postwar generation — most clearly represented in the present work by Dürrenmatt — remained committed to reason and the values of the Enlightenment. For the next generation, these values became suspect. The works discussed in the following chapters reflect this transformation as well as a broader societal need to re-examine those pivotal ideas that have determined the character of modern Western society. In this sense, they are not only literary meditations on the status of reason, knowledge, and discourse; they are also a confrontation with the intellectual foundations of modernity itself.

In order to make the discussions that follow accessible to readers with no knowledge of German, I have used English translations as available. If translations were not available I provided my own. I have included the German for those passages in which the translation did not seem adequately to capture the sense of the original.

JF
Minneapolis
February, 1992

Introduction

THE MODERN IDEA OF RATIONALITY is the legacy of attempts by seventeenth-century philosophers and scientists, particularly Descartes, Galileo, and Newton, to establish methods of inquiry designed to guarantee certainty. Their goal, which resulted in a narrowing of the concept of rationality that had been espoused by the more tolerant and skeptical humanists of the previous century, was to frame questions in such a way as to render them independent of context.[1] This new approach to knowledge was strongly influenced by developments in science. According to Hans-Georg Gadamer, it was "especially the idea of method, or of securing the path of knowledge in accord with the guiding ideal of certainty, that brought a unified meaning of knowing and knowledge to the fore." The new conception of science "grounded for the first time the narrower sense of philosophy that we have connected with the word *philosophy* since then." During the nineteenth century, "knowledge" came to be equated with scientific knowledge and "rationality" with scientific rationality.[2] This view has continued to resonate in our own time in the widespread tendency to regard "methodical," "rational," "scientific," and "objective" as synonyms. As Richard Rorty has pointed out, the obsession with method is characteristic of a secularized culture in which the scientist has replaced the priest:

> The scientist is now seen as the person who keeps humanity in touch with something beyond itself. As the universe was depersonalized, beauty (and, in time, even moral goodness) came to be thought of as 'subjective.' So truth is now thought of as the only point at which human beings are responsible to something nonhuman. A commitment to 'rationality' and to 'method' is thought to be a

[1]See Stephen Toulmin, *Cosmopolis: The Hidden Agenda of Modernity* (New York: The Free Press, 1990), esp. pp. 5-44.

[2]Hans-Georg Gadamer, *Reason in the Age of Science*, trans. Frederick G. Lawrence (Cambridge: MIT Press, 1981), pp. 152, 156.

recognition of this responsibility. The scientist becomes a moral exemplar, one who selflessly exposes himself again and again to the hardness of fact.[3]

Criticism of the epistemic hegemony of science, in the last few decades in particular, has been fueled by the rise of antifoundationalism, the view that there can be no overarching, ahistorical standard or foundation, not even an allegedly neutral scientific one, that can ground or justify claims to knowledge.[4] This idea has contributed to what has been described as a revolution in contemporary philosophy. Central to this revolution, according to Joseph Margolis, is the claim "that there is no principled demarcation between a science and the history or practice of that science" and "that there is no principled demarcation between a science and the (philosophical) theory of that science." These claims, Margolis continues, are connected with two major themes that have become prominent in philosophy: "the priority of *praxis* with respect to human speculation" and "the deep *historicity* of human existence and inquiry," the awareness that man's "cognitive and praxical concerns are oriented and limited by the historical horizon of his own particular culture."[5] In other words, as Richard Rorty has expressed it, "there is nothing deep down inside us except what we have put there ourselves, no criterion that we have not created in the course of creating a practice, no standard of rationality that is not an appeal to such a criterion, no rigorous argumentation that is not obedience to our own conventions." We are compelled to abandon the notion "that outside the haphazard and perilous experiments we perform there lies something (God, Science, Knowledge, Rationality, or Truth) which will, if only we perform the correct rituals, step in to save us."[6]

Antifoundationalism has become a staple of postmodern philosophical thinking.[7] It is implied in Derrida's critique of "logocentrism" and "the metaphysics of presence" as well as in Foucault's espousal of an "archaeological" criticism

---

[3]Richard Rorty, "Science as Solidarity," in *The Rhetoric of the Human Sciences: Language and Argument in Scholarship and Public Affairs*, eds. John S. Nelson, Allan Megill, and Donald N. McCloskey (Madison: University of Wisconsin Press, 1987), p. 38.

[4]See *Anti-Foundationalism and Practical Reasoning: Conversations between Hermeneutics and Analysis*, ed. Evan Simpson (Edmonton: Academic Printing and Publishing, 1987).

[5]Joseph Margolis, *Pragmatism without Foundations: Reconciling Realism and Relativism* (Oxford: Basil Blackwell, 1986), pp. xv, xviii. The origins of Margolis's philosophical revolution can ultimately be traced back to Nietzsche.

[6]Richard Rorty, *Consequences of Pragmatism. Essays: 1972-1980* (Minneapolis: University of Minnesota Press, 1982), pp. xlii, 208.

[7]Cf. John McGowan, who describes postmodernism as a form of cultural critique that is "resolutely antifoundationalist — eschewing all appeals to ontological or epistemological or ethical absolutes — while also proclaiming itself resolutely radical in its commitment to the transformation of the existing Western social order." *Postmodernism and Its Critics* (Ithaca: Cornell University Press, 1991), p. ix.

that "will not seek to identify the universal structures of all knowledge or of all possible moral action, but will seek to treat the instances of discourse that articulate what we think, say, and do as so many historical events."[8] For some, these developments signal the end of the ideal of enlightened reason. In his *Critique of Cynical Reason*, for example, Peter Sloterdijk declares that "all thinking has become strategy."[9] For others, such as Rorty and Jürgen Habermas, it has led not to a rejection of reason *tout court* but to a revival of another dimension of the Western tradition of rationality, the one that has its roots in the Socratic dialogue. Maintaining that "there are no constraints on inquiry save conversational ones," Rorty regards the life of reason not as the search for the proper method that would guarantee certainty, but as "Socratic conversation."[10] And Habermas presents the tradition of discursive rationality as "an alternative way out of the philosophy of the subject," contrasting it with Foucault's totalizing critique of subject-centered reason. The locus of rationality, Habermas maintains, is communication oriented to consensus. This "linguistic turn" marks a shift from the isolated, monologic Cartesian "I think" to a dialogic model that regards humans as linguistic beings caught, as Habermas has said, "in a web of communicative action."[11] As Rorty and Habermas make clear, the linguistic turn has strong political implications, for a commitment to communicative reason is fundamental to the democratic tradition and to what Habermas calls the "project of modernity."[12]

[8]Michel Foucault, "What is Enlightenment?" trans. Catherine Porter, in *The Foucault Reader*, ed. Paul Rabinow (New York: Pantheon, 1984), p. 46.

[9]Peter Sloterdijk, *Critique of Cynical Reason*, trans. Michael Eldred, Theory and History of Literature 40 (Minneapolis: University of Minnesota Press), p. xxix; *Kritik der zynischen Vernunft*, 2 vols. (Frankfurt: Suhrkamp, 1983), 1: 12.

[10]Rorty, *Consequences of Pragmatism*, pp. 164, 165.

[11]Habermas, "An Alternative Way out of the Philosophy of the Subject: Communicative versus Subject-Centered Reason," in *The Philosophical Discourse of Modernity*, trans. Frederick Lawrence (Cambridge: MIT Press, 1987), pp. 294-326; and Habermas, "Discourse Ethics: Notes on a Program of Philosophical Justification," trans. Shierry Weber Nicholsen and Christian Lenhardt, in *The Communicative Ethics Controversy*, eds. Seyla Benhabib and Fred Dallmayr (Cambridge: MIT Press, 1990), p. 97. The latter originally appeared in Habermas, *Moralbewußtsein und kommunikatives Handeln* (Frankfurt: Suhrkamp, 1983).

[12]Despite their common commitment to discourse, Habermas and Rorty do not agree on all issues. Rorty objects to the universalism implied in Habermas's theory of communicative discourse (as discussed below). Also, where Habermas regards poststructuralism as a dead end, Rorty is prepared to acknowledge the contributions of Foucault and Derrida as long as they are seen as private, as opposed to public, philosophers, a distinction Habermas does not make. Habermas discusses Rorty in Habermas, *The Philosophical Discourse of Modernity*, pp. 206-07. Rorty discusses his affinities and disagreements with Habermas in Rorty, *Contingency, Irony, Solidarity* (Cambridge: Cambridge University Press, 1989), pp. 61-69. See also Habermas, "A Philosophico-Political Profile," *New Left Review* 151 (May/June

The purpose of this book is to investigate forms of scientific and communicative rationality and their role in the quest for private and public meanings in literary texts written by six authors from Switzerland, Austria, and Germany during the last ten years or so. Because science and discourse are both integral parts of the Western tradition, the authors' preoccupation with them is also a confrontation with fundamental Western values. These works are thus not only an investigation of epistemological problems; they are also an attempt to come to terms with modernity itself.

In this introduction, I shall discuss some of the major developments during the last thirty years that have contributed to changing attitudes toward science and scientific rationality and present Habermas's theory of communicative reason as a comprehensive mode of rationality with far-reaching implications for the project of modernity. This discussion will provide a theoretical context for the literary analyses that follow.

Habermas has described the epistemic hegemony of science as "scientism," which he defines as "science's belief in itself: that is, the conviction that we can no longer understand science as *one* form of possible knowledge, but rather must identify knowledge with science."[13] This view, which is closely associated with positivism, is largely responsible for the critique of science that has gained momentum in the last three decades. The critique proceeds from an internal as well as from an external perspective. From an internal perspective, it questions whether one can legitimately speak of a method that provides privileged insight into the nature of things or of a rationality that is unique to science. According to this view, scientific method offers no guarantee of neutrality or objectivity; science is no more or no less "rational" than any other activity. From an external perspective, the critique regards scientific activity as part of a broader cultural matrix that includes social influences and ideological interests. Science, it asserts, is self-referential. Facts are theory-laden, constituted in advance by the chosen method. Hence, science does not discover reality; it constructs it. Moreover, scientific discourse is not pure or neutral, it is claimed, because all language is metaphorical; the language of science is co-extensive with that of literature. Rather than a neutral mode of inquiry dedicated to the discovery of the truth, science is said to be an ideology whose claim to be the supreme form of knowledge is the source of its power in modern society. Although it has done much to liberate us from the forces

---

1985): 71-105, and Habermas, "Die Einheit der Vernunft in der Vielheit ihrer Stimmen," *Merkur* 42 (1988): 1-14. Because he presents a well developed and interesting theory of communicative reason, I shall focus on Habermas in this introduction.

[13]Jürgen Habermas, *Knowledge and Human Interests*, trans. Jeremy J. Shapiro (Boston: Beacon Press, 1971), p. 4.

of nature, science, as a partner of technology, has also imprisoned us "in a logic of domination and degradation."[14]

One of the most influential studies of scientific method is Thomas Kuhn's *The Structure of Scientific Revolutions*, published in the early sixties. The impact of Kuhn's book can be best appreciated if his views are contrasted with those of Sir Karl Popper, perhaps the foremost philosopher of science in the twentieth century. In his *Logic of Scientific Discovery*, Popper claimed that "the growth of knowledge can be studied best by studying the growth of scientific knowledge."[15] One of his main concerns was to demarcate science from non-science by elucidating a method or "logic" that would distinguish science from other modes of discourse. According to Popper, the method of science is "the method of bold conjectures and ingenious and severe attempts to refute them." Through a process of trial and error, which is driven by "systematic *rational criticism*," inadequate theories are replaced by better ones, thus enabling science to make steady progress toward the truth (which, however, would never be attainable).[16] Popper thus regards science as the quintessentially *rational* enterprise. Scientific theories are modified or abandoned based on the force of the better argument. Even subjective factors can be neutralized, if not eliminated, he claims, by the principle of ongoing systematic criticism.[17]

All of this was called into question by Kuhn, who maintained that scientists may be persuaded to adopt a new theory for a number of reasons, not all of them rational. All scientists, he claimed, work within established paradigms that they are extremely reluctant to abandon. When they do so, they are often motivated by

---

[14]Stanley Aronowitz, *Science as Power: Discourse and Ideology in Modern Society* (Minneapolis: University of Minnesota Press, 1988), p. 341. On constructivism, the view that reality is a human construction, see Michael A. Arbib and Mary B. Hesse, *The Construction of Reality* (Cambridge: Cambridge University Press, 1986); on the notion of science as a "language game" see Jean-François Lyotard, *The Postmodern Condition: A Report on Knowledge*, trans. Geoff Bennington and Brian Massumi, Theory and History of Literature 10 (1979; Minneapolis: University of Minnesota Press, 1984); on the metaphoricity of scientific language see Arbib and Hesse, pp. 147-70 and James J. Bono, "Science, Discourse, and Literature: The Role/Rule of Metaphor in Science," in *Literature and Science: Theory and Practice,* ed. Stuart Peterfreund (Boston: Northeastern University Press, 1990), pp. 59-89; on science as ideology see Aronowitz.

[15]Karl R. Popper, Preface to the English Edition, 1958, *The Logic of Scientific Discovery* (1934; New York: Basic Books, 1959), p. 15. Italicized in the original.

[16]Popper, *Objective Knowledge: An Evolutionary Approach* (Oxford: Clarendon Press, 1972), pp. 81, 121. First quotation italicized in original.

[17]Popper's emphasis on language and his insistence that knowledge is acquired through communicative interaction show an affinity with ideas of Habermas and Rorty. His tendency to regard science as a paradigmatic mode of inquiry, however, betrays vestiges of Habermas's "scientism." It is this aspect of his work that is of interest to me here. Other aspects will be discussed more completely in chapter 1.

"personal and inarticulate aesthetic considerations" rather than by reason and logic. The acceptance of a new paradigm, or theory, is analogous to a "conversion experience"; in the final analysis, the new paradigm is accepted on faith. "There is no neutral algorithm for theory-choice," Kuhn writes, "no systematic decision procedure which, properly applied, must lead each individual in the group to the same decision."[18] Kuhn seemed to establish relativism as an inevitable and unavoidable element of scientific inquiry. Opposing paradigms, he maintained, are radically incommensurable. Individuals with different paradigms not only perceive reality differently, they actually live in different worlds. For this reason, Kuhn is skeptical of the notion that science progresses toward the truth, maintaining that there is "no theory-independent way to reconstruct phrases like 'really there'; the notion of a match between the ontology of a theory and its 'real' counterpart in nature now seems to me illusive in principle."[19] Kuhn thus suggests that science, the discipline we have traditionally regarded as paradigmatic for rationality, objectivity, and open-mindedness, is in fact governed by subjectivism and even irrationalism and that its theories have at best a tentative relation to reality. He thus helped to lay the groundwork for the antifoundationalist suspicion of any allegedly neutral method of inquiry and at the same time prepared the way for a body of opinion that came to view science as a social activity and scientific knowledge as a form of power.

The thrust of this critique is the assertion that scientific rationality is a cultural posit. Paul Feyerabend, for example, asserts not only that there is no method unique to science and that in fact "anything goes," but also that reason and rationality are simply two words "which can be connected with almost any idea or procedure" on which is then placed "a halo of excellence." The assumption that there exist "universally valid and binding standards of knowledge and action is a special case of a belief whose influence extends far beyond the domain of intellectual debate. This belief...may be formulated by saying that there exists a right way of living and that the world must be made to accept it."[20] In other words, science

---

[18]Thomas Kuhn, *The Structure of Scientific Revolutions*, 2nd ed., International Encyclopedia of Unified Science, vol.2, no.2 (Chicago: University of Chicago Press, 1970), pp. 152, 158, 200.

[19]Kuhn, pp. 202, 206. Popper rejects Kuhn's approach as an example of "the myth of the framework," the doctrine that discussion is only possible among individuals who have agreed on fundamentals. See Popper, "Normal Science and Its Dangers," in *Criticism and the Growth of Knowledge*, eds. Imre Lakatos and Alan Musgrave, Proceedings of the International Colloquium in the Philosophy of Science, London, 1965, vol. 4 (Cambridge: Cambridge University Press, 1970), pp. 51-58. See also Popper, "The Myth of the Framework," in *The Abdication of Philosophy: Philosophy and the Public Good*, ed. Eugene Freeman (LaSalle: Open Court, 1976), pp. 23-48.

[20]Paul Feyerabend, *Against Method: Outline of an Anarchistic Theory of Knowledge* (London: NLB, 1975), p. 28, and Feyerabend, *Farewell to Reason* (London: Verso, 1987), pp. 10-11.

is an ideology whose power resides in its claim to be the only reliable source of knowledge. By demarcating itself from other modes of inquiry, science defines itself as a privileged discourse and relegates other discourses to the margins. But rather than provide a neutral method for transmitting knowledge of the facts, science is motivated, as Habermas has put it, by "a cognitive interest in technical control over objectified processes." The facts are constituted in advance by the methods chosen to "discover" them. "All the answers which the empirical sciences can supply are relative to the methodical significance of the questions they raise and nothing more," Habermas insists.[21] According to this view, science, like all human activities, is self-referential; it transmits information not about the object but about our relationship to it. Even scientific experiment, which is generally assumed to contain safeguards to insure its objectivity, is, according to Stanley Aronowitz, permeated with interests. When setting up the boundaries of an experiment, the scientist must "delimit the observational field by decontextualizing the object so as to facilitate the project of predicting and controlling behavior." The experimental method is thus "informed by its presupposition of intention, that is, the control of nature and humans so that their action may be predicted." Although science portrays itself as "pure" knowledge, it has in fact become identical with technology and shares the latter's interest in domination and control.[22]

Despite its claim to be a uniquely rational enterprise, by narrowly equating scientific rationality with rationality as such, science presents "the economy in the selection of purposive-rational means" (Habermas) as the sole admissible value. All practical questions that cannot be answered technically are thought to be inaccessible to rational discussion, with the result that, as Wittgenstein wrote: "We feel that even when all *possible* scientific questions have been answered, the problems of life remain completely untouched." In this way, Habermas maintains, science unwittingly and paradoxically contributes to the growth of irrationalism in society, for

> if decisions on questions touching on the praxis of life must be pronounced as beyond any and every authority committed to rationality, then we cannot be astonished by the ultimate desperate attempt to secure socially binding precommit-

---

[21]Habermas, *Knowledge and Human Interests*, p. 309; and Habermas, "A Positivistically Bisected Rationalism," in *The Positivist Dispute in German Sociology*, trans. Glyn Adey and David Frisby (London: Heinemann, 1976), p. 209.

[22]Aronowitz, *Science as Power*, pp. 8, 329, 338, 343, and *passim*. The conflation of knowledge, technology, and domination was also asserted by members of the Frankfurt School. See especially Max Horkheimer and Theodor Adorno, *Dialectic of Enlightenment*, trans. John Cumming (1944; New York: Continuum, 1972) and Herbert Marcuse, *One-Dimensional Man: Studies in the Ideology of Advanced Industrial Society* (Boston: Beacon Press, 1964), esp. chapter 6. Aronowitz discusses the Frankfurt School in chapter 5 of *Science as Power*.

ments on practical questions institutionally by a return to the closed world of mythical images and powers.[23]

In order to preclude such a development, Habermas calls for a comprehensive rationality that would re-establish the connection of theory to practice, lost since the eighteenth century, and overcome the dualism of facts and values.

Such a comprehensive rationality is contained in Habermas's theory of communicative reason. Unlike subject-centered, Cartesian rationality, communicative rationality is rooted in the lifeworld. It is "directly implicated in social life-processes insofar as acts of mutual understanding take on the role of a mechanism for coordinating action." The reason expressed in communicative action, which Habermas defines as discourse oriented toward reaching understanding, "is mediated with the traditions, social practices, and body-centered complexes of experience that coalesce into *particular* totalities."[24] It thus restores to rational inquiry those praxical elements that, as Stephen Toulmin has pointed out, had been excluded from it by seventeenth-century rationalism: the oral, the local, the particular, and the timely.[25] Communicative rationality is so pervasive, Habermas maintains, that even a skeptic who refuses to argue cannot remove himself from the communicative web: "No matter how consistent a dropout may be, he cannot drop out of the communicative practice of everyday life, to the presuppositions of which he remains bound." As social beings, individuals have no choice but to engage in communicative action. "They do not have the option for a long-term absence from contexts of action oriented to reaching understanding. That would mean regression to the monadic isolation of strategic action — or schizophrenia and suicide. In the long run such absence is self-destructive." Communicative action is entwined with the social life of human beings. The attempt to withdraw from it leads to "an existential dead end."[26]

Discursive rationality, Habermas claims, is posited in every discourse oriented to consensus. Any individual who enters into communicative action, as opposed to strategic action (whose goal is not consensus but manipulation), makes three validity claims: to truth, rightness, and truthfulness, depending on whether the speaker is referring to something in the objective world, the shared social world, or his own subjective world. If challenged, these claims can be redeemed through rational argument. In argument, the speakers must orient themselves to what

---

[23]Jürgen Habermas, "Dogmatism, Reason, and Decision: On Theory and Praxis in Our Scientific Civilization," in *Theory and Practice*, trans. John Viertel (Boston: Beacon Press, 1973), pp. 264, 267; Ludwig Wittgenstein, *Tractatus Logico-Philosophicus*, trans. D.F. Pears and B.F. McGuinness (London: Routledge and Kegan Paul, 1961), p. 73. Cited by Habermas in *The Positivist Dispute in German Sociology*, p. 145.

[24]Habermas, "An Alternative Way out of the Philosophy of the Subject," pp. 316, 326.

[25]See Toulmin, *Cosmopolis: The Hidden Agenda of Modernity*, pp. 30-36.

[26]Habermas, "Discourse Ethics," pp. 98, 99.

Habermas calls an "ideal speech situation" characterized by reciprocity and an atmosphere free of external or internal constraints on dialogue. Although such ideal conditions are seldom, if ever, realized, they must be anticipated "counterfactually" by any individual engaged in communicative action. Hence, communication not only contributes a model for rationality, it also provides a basis for ethics. It contains norms of behavior that all participants engaged in argument leading to rational consensus must observe.[27] Moreover, the norms posited by the ideal speech situation anticipate a dialogue society in which the truth can be pursued in an atmosphere free of domination. Thus, Habermas writes, "the truth of statements is based on anticipating the realization of the good life."[28] In this way, communicative reason continues to incorporate humanity's hopes for a better society and even, if Karl-Otto Apel is to be believed, its utopian aspirations: "Human beings, as *linguistic beings* who must share *meaning and truth with fellow beings* in order to be able to think in a valid form, must at all times *anticipate counterfactually* an *ideal form of communication and hence of social interaction.*"[29]

Politically, communicative reason is closely associated with what Habermas refers to as "the public sphere," a space distinct from political institutions where "the public organizes itself as the bearer of public opinion." In modern mass democracies, the public sphere, whose origins Habermas traces back to the eighteenth century, has disintegrated. The process of making public no longer subjects matters to public reason but instead "serves the arcane policies of special

[27]By positing an "ideal speech situation" which must be observed "counterfactually" by all engaged in discourse, Habermas is attempting to avoid the charge that he is advocating a kind of foundationalism. Communicative rationality, he insists, is grounded by (historically situated) discursive *practice*. This idea has nevertheless been widely criticized. Joseph Margolis dismisses Habermas's ideas as a reincarnation of foundationalism, and Lyotard, insisting that "to speak is to fight," declares flatly: "Consensus has become an outmoded and suspect value." Richard Rorty, a more sympathetic critic, claims that Habermas's attempt to justify or legitimize communicative reason is unnecessary and that he is "scratching where it does not itch." As Rorty implies, the status of the philosophical justification of communicative reason does not affect the importance of the idea of communication for social and political questions. See Margolis, *Pragmatism without Foundations*, pp. 43-53; Lyotard, *The Postmodern Condition*, pp. 10, 66; and Rorty, "Habermas and Lyotard on Postmodernity," in *Habermas and Modernity*, ed. Richard J. Bernstein (Cambridge: MIT Press, 1985), p. 164.

[28]Habermas, "Knowledge and Human Interests: A General Perspective," in *Knowledge and Human Interests*, p. 314. See also Habermas, *The Theory of Communicative Action*, vol. 1, *Reason and the Rationalization of Society*, trans. Thomas McCarthy (Boston: Beacon Press, 1984), pp. 8-42 and 273-337; and Habermas, "Discourse Ethics," pp. 63-64. See also Thomas McCarthy, *The Critical Theory of Jürgen Habermas* (Cambridge: MIT Press, 1978), esp. pp. 272-333; and Michael Pusey, *Jürgen Habermas* (Chichester, England: Ellis Horwood, 1987), esp. pp. 69-86.

[29]Karl-Otto Apel, "Is the Ethics of the Ideal Communication Community a Utopia? On the Relationship between Ethics, Utopia, and the Critique of Utopia," trans. David Frisby, in *The Communicative Ethics Controversy*, pp. 46-47. Italics in original.

interests. "[30] Where the public sphere had originally "guaranteed the connection between rational-critical public debate and the legislative foundation of domination," it now "serves the manipulation *of* the public as much as legitimation *before* it. Critical publicity [Publizität] is supplanted by manipulative publicity."[31]

The decline of the public sphere has resulted in the privatization of life and in the attempt to solve the basic problems of existence through private meanings. According to Charles Taylor, the privatized life destroys the solidarity necessary for the collective formation of society. The recreation of public meanings, the prerequisite for this collective work, requires the establishment of what Taylor calls a "dialogue society," the notion of "a society in public dialogue."[32] It requires genuine democratization, for democracy, as John Dewey has said, is not just "a kind of political mechanism that will work as long as citizens [are] reasonably faithful in performing political duties." It is a way of life whose "heart and final guarantee" lies "in free gatherings of neighbors on the street corner to discuss back and forth what is read in uncensored news of the day, and in gatherings of friends in the living rooms of houses and apartments to converse freely with one another." Democracy, Dewey maintains, is a moral idea, and like Habermas, he associates this moral dimension with the possibility of free and unrestricted communication.[33]

Communicative reason is thus entwined with the project of modernity, whose aim, according to Habermas, is to foster emancipation by creating possibilities for communicative interaction free of domination. Despite the decline of the

---

[30]Habermas, "The Public Sphere: An Encyclopedia Article (1964)," trans. Sara Lennox and Frank Lennox, *New German Critique* 1.3 (1974): 50, 55. (Originally published in *Fischer Lexikon: Staat und Politik* [Frankfurt: Fischer, 1964], pp. 220-26).

[31]Habermas, *Structural Transformation of the Public Sphere: An Inquiry into a Category of Bourgeois Society*, trans. Thomas Burger and Frederick Lawrence (Cambridge: MIT Press, 1989), pp. 177-78. (Originally published 1962.) Habermas has been criticized for basing his notion of the public sphere on an idealized ahistorical model and of applying this model to modern society. But as Peter Hohendahl has pointed out, this "ideal model is necessary for describing diachronic changes." Habermas's model of the public sphere "provides a paradigm for analyzing historical change, while also serving as a normative category for political critique. In order to prevent a decline to a merely descriptive concept of public opinion, he insists on its emphatic use, although he admits the irreversibility of the historical processes involved." "Critical Theory, Public Sphere, and Culture: Jürgen Habermas and His Critics," trans. Marc Silverman, in Hohendahl, *The Institution of Criticism* (Ithaca: Cornell University Press, 1982), p. 246.

[32]Charles Taylor, "From Marxism to the Dialogue Society," in *From Culture to Revolution: The Slant Symposium 1967*, ed. Terry Eagleton and Brian Wicker (London: Sheed and Ward, 1968), pp. 176-77 and *passim*.

[33]John Dewey, "Creative Democracy — The Task Before Us," in Dewey, *The Later Works*, 17 vols., ed. Jo Ann Boydston (Carbondale, Illinois: Southern Illinois University Press, 1988), 14: 225, 227, 228.

"classical" public sphere (the eighteenth-century model), the ultimate fate of this project has not yet been determined, for, Habermas insists, the "release of a potential for reason embedded in communicative action is a world-historical process." He remains convinced "that a humane collective life depends on the vulnerable forms of innovation-bearing, reciprocal and unforcedly egalitarian everyday communication." The locus of discourse may have shifted in modern society to marginalized groups, but, Habermas claims, it is still present:

> I would not speak of 'communicative rationalization' if, in the last two hundred years of European and American history, in the last forty years of the national liberation movements, and despite all catastrophes, a piece of 'existing reason,' as Hegel would have put it, were not nevertheless also recognizable — in the bourgeois emancipation movements, no less than in the workers' movement, today in feminism, in cultural revolts, in ecological and pacifist forms of resistance, etc.[34]

An expansion of "reciprocal and unforcedly egalitarian everyday communication" would counteract the hegemony of science and what Habermas calls "the scientization of politics" by subjecting science to social and ethical constraints: "A scientized society could constitute itself as a rational one only to the extent that science and technology are mediated with the conduct of life through the minds of its citizens."[35] The mediation of science through discursive action is also the goal of what Marcus Raskin and Herbert Bernstein refer to as "reconstructive knowledge." Raskin and Bernstein subscribe to the view that "scientific descriptions of the world and universe" are "social and rhetorical myths of persuasion. Therefore, because they are social constructions and because they construct our image of the world, they may be judged ethically." This ethical undertaking requires free and unrestricted dialogue. The "dialogic method," Raskin and Bernstein maintain, "creates new understandings and relationships while allowing for a set of inquiries which will cause the person and group to rethink their methods, conclusions, or views." Reconstructive knowledge thus depends on "the generation of discourse and the fashioning of actions which transform the relationship of knowledge to the distribution of power in society."[36] This transformation can bring about new, more authentic public meanings.

Although not all of the authors discussed in the following chapters would agree with Raskin and Bernstein that scientific descriptions of the world are little more than "social and rhetorical myths of persuasion," their works can nevertheless be

---

[34]Habermas, "A Philosophico-Political Profile," pp. 82, 101, 102.

[35]Habermas, "The Scientization of Politics and Public Opinion," in *Towards a Rational Society: Student Protest, Science, and Politics*, trans. Jeremy Shapiro (Boston: Beacon Press, 1970), pp. 79-80.

[36]Marcus G. Raskin and Herbert J. Bernstein, *New Ways of Knowing: The Sciences, Society, and Reconstructive Knowledge* (Totowa, New Jersey: Rowman and Littlefield, 1987), pp. 78, 279, 282.

seen as contributing to a reconstructive process, broadly construed. The preoccupation with science and scientific rationality in these books reflects a need to re-evaluate science's role in society either by re-asserting its epistemic hegemony or by calling for new public meanings to replace those of the dominant, scientific ideology. Friedrich Dürrenmatt, and to some extent Rolf Hochhuth, continue to exhibit a positive attitude toward science that might even be described, in Habermas's sense, as scientistic. Dürrenmatt's epistemological model is provided by Sir Karl Popper's theory of scientific method. By asserting that the final truth can never be discovered but that knowledge can nevertheless grow by way of systematic rational criticism, Popper elucidated a theory that was able to accommodate Dürrenmatt's innate skepticism as well as his instinctive commitment to reason.

Following Popper, Dürrenmatt also applied these scientific ideas to politics, where they became the foundation for his advocacy of liberal democracy: like science, political institutions should be founded on the principle of uninhibited critical discourse. Thus, despite its "scientistic" elements, Dürrenmatt's outlook, like Popper's, contains a communicative element that clearly bears affinities to Habermas's notion of discursive rationality.[37] His plays are also a part of this discursive process. By addressing topical issues, they contribute to the creation of new public meanings and thus to the viability of the public sphere.[38] Rolf Hochhuth subscribes to a similar philosophy, but as my analysis of his *Judith* shows, his commitment to discursive rationality is at best a fragile one. His heroine rejects the path of discourse and succumbs to the nostalgia for final certainties.

In the works of Thomas Bernhard, Gerhard Roth, Peter Sloterdijk, and Christoph Ransmayr, science and scientific rationality are frequently the object of a vociferous critique that recalls the critical analyses of Habermas, Kuhn, Feyerabend, or Aronowitz. For Roth, Sloterdijk, and Ransmayr in particular, the epistemic hegemony of science has resulted in the obliteration of deeper public meanings; it has led to the creation of a technological world that is, in Charles Taylor's words, "opaque to the sacred."[39] In the works of all four writers, the suspicion of scientific rationality, which is frequently equated with positivism or technical instrumentality, is extended to communicative rationality as well. Peter Sloterdijk, for example, has unequivocally rejected Habermas's notion of an ideal

[37]Especially in his early work, such as his contributions to *The Positivist Dispute in German Sociology*, Habermas seemed reluctant to acknowledge the affinities between his notion of discursive rationality and Popper's.

[38]Throughout this book, I employ the term "public sphere," following Habermas's own practice, as a normative category. It designates an admittedly idealized space where discourse can take place free of domination and where new public meanings can be articulated. See note 31 above.

[39]Taylor, pp. 165-66.

speech community as an example of "foolish idealism" that is ripe for ridicule: "To preserve the healing fiction of a free dialogue is one of the last tasks of philosophy."[40] The protagonists in these works frequently withdraw from the social world and its communicative web and attempt to find private meanings to replace public ones that are regarded as unauthentic. But as a solution to the collapse of public meanings, such efforts are often counterproductive, a fact that is demonstrated most dramatically in the novels of Thomas Bernhard, whose protagonists retreat to a subjective universe but also to a life of neurotic isolation. As Taylor has stressed,

> [i]t is a cartesian-derived error to believe that man can define himself without reference to anything outside. Men decide who they are in terms of their relation to outside reality, and more particularly in terms of that outside reality to which they are related in [a] very basic way...*that from which one has received and to which one gives in return.*[41]

The works of these four authors are thus symptomatic of a fundamental societal malaise. They demonstrate both the difficulty of life in a society where the recipient/donor relationship between individual and community has collapsed as well as the impossibility of the alternative: a life of insular interiority. In these works, communicative action remains a peripheral phenomenon; it is not presented as a viable alternative to the protagonists' solitary quest for knowledge, meaning, and identity. It is this fact, perhaps more than any other, that constitutes their authors' pessimistic judgment on the fate of the project of modernity.

---

[40]Peter Sloterdijk, *Critique of Cynical Reason*, p. 14; *Kritik der zynischen Vernunft*, 1: 50.

[41]Taylor, p. 160. Italics in original.

1 Saving Reason: Friedrich Dürrenmatt and the Model of Science

IN AN INTERVIEW IN DECEMBER 1990, ten days before his death, Friedrich Dürrenmatt (1921-1990) recalled the two themes that had dominated his work for the last forty years. The first was the view of human events as "unpredictable," "grotesque," and "absurd"; the second was an ongoing commitment to reason and enlightenment that, as Dürrenmatt made clear in the interview, owed its inspiration and abiding vitality to the philosophy of Kant: "My goal is enlightenment. I would like human beings to free themselves from their self-imposed immaturity through thinking."[1] These two themes are closely related, for one of Dürrenmatt's aims was to investigate what it means to think and act "reasonably" in a world that has become "a riddle of misfortune."[2] During the 1960s and 1970s, as a result of his encounter with the critical epistemologies of Kant, Hans Vaihinger, Alexander Wittenberg, and Sir Karl Popper, Dürrenmatt adopted a concept of rationality that equates "reasonable" with "critical" and "scientific." The most important of these thinkers for Dürrenmatt was Karl Popper, whose theory of scientific method accommodated the two currents of Dürrenmatt's own thought. While acknowledging the impossibility of final knowledge or certainty, Popper's evolutionary

[1]"Mein Engagement gilt der Aufklärung. Ich möchte, daß die Menschen sich aus ihrer selbstverschuldeten Unmündigkeit befreien, indem sie denken." "Man stirbt. Und plötzlich blickt man zum Mond. Zeit-Gespräch mit Friedrich Dürrenmatt" [One Dies. And Suddenly One Looks at the Moon. Zeit Conversation with Friedrich Dürrenmatt], interview with Michael Haller, Die Zeit 28 December 1990: 17-18. The interview took place on December 3, 4, and 5. Dürrenmatt also acknowledged his debt to Kant in a speech given a month earlier and published posthumously: "But a fearless reason is the only thing that will be available to us in the future that might possibly enable us to withstand it; the only thing that, in accordance with Kant's hope, would enable us to pull ourselves out of disaster by our own hair." Kants Hoffnung: Zwei politische Reden. Zwei Gedichte aus dem Nachlaß [Kant's Hope: Two Political Speeches. Two Posthumous Poems] (Zürich: Diogenes, 1991), p. 48. Unless otherwise indicated, all translations throughout are my own.

[2]Dürrenmatt, Werkausgabe in dreißig Bänden [Collected Works in Thirty Volumes] (Zürich: Diogenes, 1980), 24: 63. Further references to Werkausgabe will be indicated parenthetically by volume and page number in the text.

epistemology asserts that knowledge can grow and even progress towards the truth. His theory thus enabled Dürrenmatt to "save" reason while at the same time acknowledging its limitations. It also provided theoretical support for Dürrenmatt's political views, particularly for his commitment to liberalism.

I shall begin with an analysis of epistemological questions, first in Dürrenmatt's essays and speeches and then in three works of fiction written during the 1980s. I shall conclude with a discussion of his political philosophy and an analysis of communication in one of his early comedies.

In the preface to his 1977 speech "Über Toleranz" [On Tolerance], Dürrenmatt mentions six works dealing with epistemological questions that had an influence on this thinking: Kant's *Critique of Pure Reason*, Hans Vaihinger's *The Philosophy of As-If*, Alexander Wittenberg's *Vom Denken in Begriffen* [On Conceptual Thinking], Arthur Eddington's *Philosophy of Physical Science*, and Karl Popper's *Objective Knowledge* and *The Open Society and Its Enemies*.[3] These books are characterized by a skeptical attitude toward metaphysical speculation and a vigorously anti-dogmatic stance, dogmatism having been described by Kant as "the presumption that it is possible to make any progress with pure (philosophical) knowledge, consisting of concepts, and guided by principles, such as reason has long been in the habit of employing, without first enquiring in what way, and by

---

[3]*Werkausgabe in dreißig Bänden*, 27: 127-28. The following works in particular show the influence of one or more of these thinkers: *Zusammenhänge: Essay über Israel* [Connections: Essay on Israel] (1975) (*Werkausgabe*, vol. 29), "Überlegungen zum Gesetz der großen Zahl" [Reflections on the Law of Large Quantities] (1976-77), "Über Toleranz" [On Tolerance] (1977), and "Albert Einstein" (1979) (all three in *Werkausgabe*, vol. 27); the *Nachgedanken* [After-Thoughts] appended to the Israel essay in 1980 (vol. 29); "Kunst und Wissenschaft oder Platon oder Einfall, Vision und Idee oder Die Schwierigkeit einer Anrede oder Anfang und Ende einer Rede" [Art and Science or Plato or Insight, Vision, and Idea or The Difficulty of a Salutation or Beginning and End of a Speech] (1984); and "Georg Büchner und der Satz vom Grunde. Dankesrede zum Georg-Büchner-Preis 1986 der Deutschen Akademie für Sprache und Dichtung" [Georg Büchner and the Proposition on Causality. Speech in Gratitude for the 1986 Georg Büchner Prize of the German Academy for Language and Literature] (1986), both in Dürrenmatt, *Versuche* [Essays] (Zürich: Diogenes, 1988).

Mona Knapp and Gerhard P. Knapp briefly discuss the influence of Popper in Dürrenmatt's *Monstervortrag über Gerechtigkeit und Recht* [Monster Lecture on Justice and Law] (1969). See their "Recht — Gerechtigkeit — Politik. Zur Genese der Begriffe im Werk Friedrich Dürrenmatts," in *Friedrich Dürrenmatt II*, ed. Heinz Ludwig Arnold, text + kritik 56 (Munich: edition text + kritik, 1977), pp. 32-33. In his book on Dürrenmatt, Gerhard P. Knapp acknowledges the influence of Vaihinger as well as the "scientific influences" of Popper and Eddington on Dürrenmatt's thinking, but does not examine these influences systematically. See Knapp, *Friedrich Dürrenmatt*, Sammlung Metzler 196 (Stuttgart: Metzler, 1980), p. 106. A systematic investigation of scientific thinking in Dürrenmatt's detective fiction can be found in A. M. Wright, "Scientific Method and Rationality in Dürrenmatt," *German Life and Letters* NS 35 (1981): 64-72. The influence of scientific thinking on Dürrenmatt's detective fiction has also been noted by Jan Knopf, *Friedrich Dürrenmatt*, 3rd ed., Autorenbücher 3 (Munich: Beck, 1980), pp. 46-63.

what right, it has come possessed of them."[4] All of these thinkers follow Kant in assuming a critical attitude toward speculative reason and conceptual language. Among them, it was Vaihinger, Wittenberg, and especially Popper who exerted the greatest influence on Dürrenmatt.

Vaihinger and Wittenberg both developed theories of discursive thought whose main focus was the mind's ability to employ concepts and ideas for purely provisional and expedient purposes. Vaihinger calls such concepts "fictions" or "fruitful errors." As a necessary tool of the mind, a fiction is "a mere auxiliary construct, a circuitous approach, a scaffolding afterwards to be demolished"; it is justifiable, if not verifiable.[5] In a similar manner, Wittenberg sets out to criticize our "fantastic trust in what is *thinkable*" and our "thoughtless faith in concepts," which lead us to accept language as a reliable mirror of reality. In an approach similar to Vaihinger's, Wittenberg proposes a functional use of certain concepts, called "*epistemological incisions*," which can be used provisionally to examine other conceptual complexes. Realizing that they are merely expedient, we can nevertheless employ such concepts as part of an investigation, he maintains, as if they had been given to us absolutely.[6] Vaihinger and Wittenberg both view "fictions" and "epistemological incisions" as tools that the mind uses for solving practical problems. Both are skeptical of the mind's ability to provide ultimate answers or to grasp the essence of things. "The wish to understand the world is not only unrealizable," Vaihinger asserts, "but also it is a very stupid wish."[7] Questions of ultimate truth are indifferent; logical systems do not imply truth. According to Wittenberg: "The objective fact that we are bound to certain matrices of meaning must be carefully separated from transcendental hypotheses about truth as well as from the claim to supernatural guarantees for thought."[8] For Vaihinger, truth is "merely the most expedient type of error. It is an error to suppose that an absolute truth, an absolute criterion of knowledge and behaviour, can be discovered."[9]

Similar ideas are found in the writings of Karl Popper. Like Vaihinger and Wittenberg, Popper stresses the tentative, "fictional" nature of logical constructs,

---

[4]Immanuel Kant, Preface to the Second Edition, *Critique of Pure Reason*, trans. F. Max Müller (Garden City: Anchor, 1966), p. xlii.

[5]Hans Vaihinger, *The Philosophy of "As If": A System of the Theoretical, Practical and Religious Fictions of Mankind*, trans. C. K. Ogden, 2nd ed. (London: Routledge and Keegan Paul, 1935), pp. 45, 88.

[6]Alexander Israel Wittenberg, *Vom Denken in Begriffen: Mathematik als Experiment des reinen Denkens* (Basel: Birkhäuser, 1957), pp. 20, 21, 245, 247.

[7]Vaihinger, p. 171.

[8]Wittenberg, p. 300.

[9]Vaihinger, p. 84.

in this case, of scientific theories, whose genesis he regards as intuitive rather than as logically necessary. Popper maintains "that there is no such thing as a logical method of having new ideas" and freely concedes "that every discovery contains 'an irrational element,' or 'a creative intuition.'"[10] This intuitive element is essential to the growth of scientific knowledge. *"The method of science is the method of bold conjectures and ingenious and severe attempts to refute them,"* he writes.[11] Science is not concerned with certainties or truth but with *falsifiable* theories and hypotheses:

> But this view of scientific method means that in science there is no *'knowledge'*...in the sense which implies finality; in science, we never have sufficient reason for the belief that we have attained the truth....In the empirical sciences...proofs do not occur, if we mean by 'proof' an argument which establishes once and for ever the truth of a theory. (What may occur, however, are refutations of scientific theories).[12]

Knowledge grows, in science and elsewhere, "through error-elimination by way of systematic *rational criticism*"; truth is not the ultimate goal but a "regulative idea."[13] Through this process of criticism and error-elimination we can achieve "objective knowledge": "Thus the elimination of error leads to the objective growth of our knowledge — of knowledge in the objective sense. It leads to the growth of objective verisimilitude: it makes possible the approximation to (absolute) truth."[14]

Vaihinger, Wittenberg, and Popper provided a philosophical justification for Dürrenmatt's instinctive distrust of ideologies. Dogmatic ideologies, Dürrenmatt maintains, are based on the erroneous belief in the identity of language, thought, and reality. In a passage that clearly betrays the influence of Wittenberg, he locates the "problem of language" in the fact "that language merely *names* the 'reality' outside of language. It is not identical with it....because naming and being, language and being, thinking and being are not the same" (29: 101). Ideologies are "linguistic systems...that refer to certain states of affairs but that all too easily take

---

[10]Karl R. Popper, "Scientific Method," in *Popper: Selections*, ed. David Miller (Princeton: Princeton University Press, 1985), p. 134. Reprinted from Popper, *The Logic of Scientific Discovery* (New York: Basic Books, 1959), p. 32.

[11]Popper, *Objective Knowledge: An Evolutionary Approach* (Oxford: Clarendon Press, 1972), p. 81. Italics in original.

[12]Popper, *The Open Society and Its Enemies*, 5th ed., 2 vols. (Princeton: Princeton University Press, 1966), 2: 12-13. Eddington's conception of scientific method is similar to Popper's: "We are not making a series of shots at ultimate truth, which may hit or miss." Arthur Eddington, *The Philosophy of Physical Science* (Cambridge: Cambridge University Press; New York: Macmillan, 1939), p. 5.

[13]Popper, *Objective Knowledge*, pp. 120, 121.

[14]*Objective Knowledge*, p. 126.

themselves to be identical with these states of affairs" (29: 96). As a conceptual system, an ideology may be true in context, as measured against itself [*in sich*]; but it does not follow that it is also true absolutely [*an sich*]. An ideology has no claim to truth. "An ideology is not a science" (29: 161), Dürrenmatt insists. Following Popper, he maintains that a true scientist regards every theory "as a conception, a sketch, a working hypothesis, not as 'truth'" (14: 157). Scientific theories can at best merely approach the truth; they are approximations (14: 159).[15] To the extent that it claims to be true, an ideology is a "dogma," to which empirical observations must conform (14: 157); it ceases to be a science and becomes a religion.[16] A belief in the identity of language and being, Dürrenmatt concludes, is little more than "superstition" (29: 108).

Popper demarcates science from non-science by maintaining that scientific theories are always potentially falsifiable whereas non-scientific statements are not. This demarcation principle resonates in a number of Dürrenmatt's texts, where it becomes a touchstone for the intellectual viability of any idea.[17] This is apparent in two recent essays. In "Georg Büchner und der Satz vom Grunde" [Georg Büchner and the Proposition on Causality] (1986), he contrasts Büchner's search for the foundation of all creation in "the law of beauty" with the method of modern science, which, aware of "the implacable law of evolution," eschews the search for the final truth and continually tests its interpretations against reality, progressing, he says in genuinely Popperian language, "from error to error."[18] Similarly, in "Kunst und Wissenschaft" [Art and Science] (1984), he criticizes Plato's thinking as unscientific based on Popper's demarcation. According to Dürrenmatt,

---

[15]They have, as Dürrenmatt states, "einen Annäherungswert" (14: 159), a value as approximations rather than as attempts to formulate the truth once and for all.

[16]This type of thinking is responsible for Dürrenmatt's frequent and occasionally overwrought polemics against Marxism: "Hegel and Marx...created a new religion whose attraction lies in the fact that it presents itself as scientific" (29: 175). As a religion, such an ideology requires not criticism from its adherents, but faith. "But the classical Marxist holds fast to the exclusiveness of his conception. He cannot get on without the belief that Marxism is the 'truth'" (14: 159). Although he acknowledges Marxism's contributions to our understanding of the relationship between the individual and society, he rejects its claims to be dogmatically true (see 28: 137). Like any other theory, Marxism should be regarded as "a tentative working hypothesis" (29: 165) that is subject to criticism and eventual revision, if necessary. "One must also be a Marxist scientifically" (29: 195), he maintains. In a recent speech, he praised Soviet president Mikhail Gorbachev for recognizing Marxist-Leninism as a "working hypothesis" that can now be "dropped." See Dürrenmatt, *Kants Hoffnung: Zwei politische Reden. Zwei Gedichte aus dem Nachlaß*, pp. 46-47.

[17]This procedure has also been employed by Popper himself. Based on this principle of demarcation, he condemns both Marxism and psychoanalysis as unscientific. See Popper, "The Problem of Demarcation," in *Popper: Selections*, pp. 127-28.

[18]*Versuche*, pp. 62, 65, 66.

Plato "burdened language with being"; he assumed that language was "truth."[19] In contrast to scientific theories, which are "verifiable or falsifiable," Plato's ideas are neither "refutable nor provable" (87).[20] Plato thus belongs not to the domain of science but to that of art.[21] He was, says Dürrenmatt, the "first modern writer [Schriftsteller]."[22]

This demarcation principle is also at work in Dürrenmatt's fiction, which can be interpreted as an ongoing demonstration of the folly of "unscientific" thought and action. This can be shown in three recent prose works. Like most of Dürrenmatt's works, these books focus on the inscrutability of the world and the difficulty, if not impossibility, of planned, rational action. But here the difficulty of attaining certain knowledge is complicated by an additional element: the unreliability of perception and the ambivalence of the subject itself. In these works, the individual's perception of the world appears as a creation of his or her own mind; "knowledge" is exposed as subjective projection. This subjectivism underscores the need for greater epistemological circumspection, but like so many of Dürrenmatt's other figures, the protagonists of these works assume that their perception of the world or their theories about the world are true. They thus disregard the two most important principles of Dürrenmatt's "scientific" epistemology: namely, that the final truth can never be discovered and that theories are at best tentative hypotheses or intuitive conjectures.

The unreliability of perception is the theme of *Minotaurus: Eine Ballade* [Minotaur: A Ballad] (1985), a short work which Dürrenmatt described as "an important text."[23] Unlike his Greek prototype, Dürrenmatt's mythical creature is not a vicious beast but a helpless creature struggling to orient himself in a complex world. The crimes he commits are a consequence of perceptual and epistemological confusion, not malevolence. Trapped within a labyrinth of mirrors whose reflections obey his every movement, the minotaur at first believes he is a god with dominion over all he surveys. Eventually, however, he comes to realize that the other creatures he sees are merely reflections of himself:

> He fell back. His mirror image did likewise, and gradually it dawned on him that he was opposite himself. He attempted to flee, but wherever he turned, he always

---

[19]*Versuche*, p. 83.

[20]According to Popper, however, scientific theories are always falsifiable but they are never verifiable, if the latter is taken to mean "proven to be true once and for all."

[21]Although the German word "Wissenschaft" is broader in meaning than the English word "science," I have generally used the two terms interchangeably here, since both imply a mode of inquiry characterized by a certain rigor of method.

[22]*Versuche*, p. 95.

[23]Dürrenmatt, "Das 'Labyrinth' oder Über die Grenzen des Menschseins." Interview with Michael Haller in Dürrenmatt, *Über die Grenzen* (Zürich: pendo-verlag, 1990), p. 105.

stood opposite himself. He was walled in by himself. Everywhere he was himself; endlessly he was himself.[24]

The minotaur's confrontation with his reflection is a metaphor for the subjectivism and self-referentiality inherent in all quests for knowledge. But as he soon discovers, the notion that reality is merely a projection of consciousness is just as precarious as the belief that the mind accurately "reflects" the truth of an independently existing world. Disguised as a minotaur, Theseus kills the disoriented creature, who mistakes his murderer for his own reflection.

The unmasking of perception as self-perception and of knowledge as subjective projection is also the theme of *The Assignment, Or On the Observing of the Observer of the Observers: Novelle in Twenty-Four Sentences* [*Der Auftrag oder Vom Beobachten des Beobachters der Beobachter: Novelle in vierundzwanzig Sätzen*] (1986). Otto von Lambert asks the filmmaker F to "reconstruct" the death of his wife Tina, who left him and was found murdered in the North African desert. F accepts the assignment only to discover that the dead woman is not Tina but a Danish journalist to whom Tina, who never left the country, had lent her passport and her red fur coat. In Africa, F encounters Polyphem, a crazed cameraman who wants to film F being murdered, but as luck would have it his plan is upset by a political coup and she (the filmmaker F) is saved. In the meantime, Tina, having ended her affair with a local painter, has reconciled herself with her husband. When, following a tip in Tina's diary, F visited the painter's studio before leaving for Africa, she narrowly missed Tina, who quickly slipped out of the building. F's trip to Africa was unnecessary and could have been avoided had she been more observant. So close to the truth, she nevertheless allowed it to escape her grasp.

F's search for Tina quickly changes from an attempt to "reconstruct" reality to a quest for her own identity. In the painter's studio, she believes she recognizes herself in a painting of Frau von Lambert, and while in Africa she impulsively buys a red fur coat such as that worn by Tina. Later, when viewing a film of the Danish journalist, she identifies with the murdered woman, and towards the end of the novella she asks whether the truth she has been seeking is not in fact the truth about herself.[25] The question of identity is also the subject of F's conversation early in the novella with the logician D (in whom the reader easily recognizes Dürrenmatt himself). Human beings, he informs her, are never identical with themselves because they are constantly changing with the passage of time (*Assignment* 14-15; *Auftrag* 18). Every self, F concludes, is therefore a construct, "a collective term for all the selves gathered up in the past" (*Assignment* 25;

---

[24]Dürrenmatt, *Minotaurus: Eine Ballade* (Zürich: Diogenes, 1985), p. 40.

[25]Dürrenmatt, *The Assignment, Or On the Observing of the Observer of the Observers: Novelle in Twenty-Four Sentences*, trans. Joel Agee (New York: Random House, 1988), pp. 120-21; *Der Auftrag oder Vom Beobachten des Beobachters der Beobachter: Novelle in vierundzwanzig Sätzen* (Zürich: Diogenes, 1986), p. 125. Further references will be indicated in the text.

Auftrag 28). When D continues that every observation is an attempt to objectify, to assign meaning, it is clear that this objectification and this meaning are influenced by the fluctuating positions of the observer. Like the minotaur pondering his own reflection in the mirrors surrounding him, F learns that every observation, every attempt to find the truth, is self-referential; it must of necessity lead back to the self.

Like the minotaur, F had believed that the relationship between subject and object was unproblematic and that the truth was manifest. Before accepting von Lambert's assignment, she had been engaged in a film project whose goal was the creation of a "total portrait" of the planet, which she hoped to achieve by splicing together "random scenes" into a whole (*Assignment* 5; *Auftrag* 10). In her hubris, she is closely related to her antagonist in the novella, Polyphem, who plans to visualize "a crystallized reality" by capturing actions in photographs as brief as one-thousandth of second (*Assignment* 109; *Auftrag* 112). Convinced of his ability thus to perceive and know the world, Polyphem, like the ill-fated minotaur, thinks himself a god. God, he says, is "pure observation"; He is "unsullied by his creation" (*Assignment* 107; *Auftrag* 110-11). F and Polyphem are thus united in their conviction that reality can be known, F by producing a "total" picture of it, Polyphem by reducing it to its essentials. But just as F discovered that observation is always influenced by subjective factors, Polyphem discovers that it is impossible to remove oneself from the world and assume the position of an aloof, "pure" observer: he himself is being observed by two computer-driven satellites, and an observed god, he says, is no longer a god.

In Dürrenmatt's later works, God frequently appears as a metaphor for the final and ultimately unknowable answer to all existential questions. He is the entity in whom observation and knowledge are one; for God, to observe is to know. Whether He exists or not is for the later Dürrenmatt a matter of indifference; He is of no consequence for humanity. Our idea of God, he maintains, is a daring linguistic conception, a fiction, whose truth cannot be demonstrated. Moreover, the truth value of this fiction is unimportant (29: 105). It is a tool that the mind uses to come to terms with reality, for, Dürrenmatt insists, the human mind operates with conceptions, not with truth.[26] Thus, according to the logician D,

---

[26]"...der menschliche Geist verhält sich konzipierend, nicht 'wahr,' er dringt in die 'Wahrheit' vermittels Konzeptionen, er ist nicht identisch mit der Wahrheit" (29: 105). Jan Knopf has been highly critical of assertions of this kind, claiming that Dürrenmatt severs the necessary connection between language and reality. The result is "that what appears in the formulations is nothing but language, to which no extra-linguistic image corresponds: language has freed itself from objects and no longer expresses them linguistically. The statement about something — that has broken down." Dürrenmatt's notion of "conceptions," he maintains, is subjective, relativistic, and unscientific. This is a misrepresentation of Dürrenmatt's position. By stressing the notion of "conceptions," Dürrenmatt is emphasizing the creative, intuitive element involved in our acquisition of knowledge (cf. Vaihinger's "fictions," Wittenberg's "epistemological incisions," and Popper's "bold conjectures"). But he makes it clear that these conceptions are not to be regarded as absolute (i.e. true). Like any hypothesis, a conception can be upheld only as long as it has not been refuted by (real)

God is dead. He lives on only "as an abstract principle," as an "axiom of faith without any roots in human understanding" (*Assignment* 19-20; *Auftrag* 23-24). God belongs to the realm of logic, whose relationship to reality is completely arbitrary and which is therefore conveniently safe, D says, "from every sort of existential mishap" (*Assignment* 15; *Auftrag* 18).

In the 1989 novel *Durcheinandertal* [Muddle Valley], this "safe" logical domain is represented by theology. Moses Melker is a successful theologian who developed an ingenious and self-serving theology that proclaims the rich to be the recipients of God's grace. He has become wealthy from his books and by inheriting from his wives, all three of whom he murdered along with a fourth woman, whom he also raped in the process. Melker attempts to do with theology what F and Polyphem attempted with their cameras: to assume a position of "pure observation." For Melker, this means concocting an overarching theory to explain away contradictions and supply an ultimate meaning for his life. He uses theology, which he describes as "a board across an abyss," to justify his own wantonness and greed: "As poor Moses, the Kingdom of Heaven belonged to him. As rich Moses, it was awarded to him through grace."[27]

Melker's theology is a good example of a non-falsifiable and therefore "unscientific" theory. He is able to incorporate any godless and thus potentially falsifying behavior, including murder, rape, and exploitation, into his theory without logical contradiction. Melker eventually comes to understand the absurdity of this undertaking: "It [his theology] collapsed upon itself; it stumbled into the trap set by its own concepts. It thought of God as perfect and of the world as imperfect. The whole thing a purely mental construct with no connection to reality..." (174). Despite internal logical consistency, Melker implies, no theory can provide an absolutely secure foundation for knowledge, because any such theory, as a product of human activity, is subject to the same capriciousness it attempts to explain away. Melker is trapped in the same circularity we encountered in the previously discussed works. If God is his invention, he reasons, then so is the world, and there must therefore also be other gods and other worlds invented by others, so that the world is the sum of innumerable universes, each the product of a different mind (cf. 175). We are back to the situation of the minotaur: "Everywhere he was himself; endlessly he was himself."

Durcheinandertal demonstrates the dangers of "unscientific" attempts to equate language with being or theories with truth. In *Turmbau: Stoffe IV-IX* [Construction

---

contrary evidence; it is at best a tentative approximation to truth. Dürrenmatt condemns as "sophistic" (29: 110) any use of language, as for example in dogmatic ideologies, that is indifferent to reality, insisting that one must live "in a state of tension with this reality; in the tension between language and what is meant" (29: 111). See Jan Knopf, "Sprachmächtigkeiten," in *Facetten: Studien zum 60. Geburtstag Friedrich Dürrenmatts*, eds. Gerhard P. Knapp and Gerd Lambroisse (Bern: Peter Lang, 1981). p. 69. See also Knopf, *Friedrich Dürrenmatt*, pp. 156-59 and Gerhard P. Knapp, *Friedrich Dürrenmatt*, p. 110.

[27]Dürrenmatt, *Durcheinandertal* (Zürich: Diogenes, 1989), pp. 17, 173.

of the Tower: Subject Matter IV-IX] (1990), the second volume of his account of
his literary development, Dürrenmatt attempted to show that all quests for certainty
must fail because of the inevitable entwinement of logic and faith. In a section of
the book entitled "Die Brücke" [The Bridge], he ponders the various reasons that
might have convinced the young F.D. to cross or not to cross the Kirchenfeld
Bridge in Bern in 1943. One of these fictional selves, who has decided to lead a
completely logical life, will cross the bridge only if he is absolutely certain that it
will not collapse. He hopes in this way to unite logic and reality. This F.D.,
Dürrenmatt reports, is standing before the Kirchenfeld Bridge to this day. For even
if he constructed countless bridges, he would never succeed in building one that
would be absolutely safe. The life based on logic would thus become a life
motivated by faith, the faith that there must be an absolutely safe bridge.[28]

In Dürrenmatt's account, the bridge becomes a metaphor for the shakiness of
foundationalism, the notion that there can be logical or metaphysical guarantees for
knowledge claims. Although it seems to be safe, the bridge, like all bridges, could
conceivably collapse. Crossing it requires, as Dürrenmatt says, "a grain of
faith."[29] In other words, there can be no secure logical or metaphysical foundations. Our knowledge, he says, is hypothetical, and like the mathematical bridge
between one and zero that never reaches zero, our hypotheses can never arrive at
absolute truth.[30]

Epistemological insights of this kind also influenced Dürrenmatt's political
outlook. Once again, science, and particularly the thought of Karl Popper, occupy
a central position in Dürrenmatt's texts, especially in those written in the late
1970s.

Popper describes the scientific approach to social and political questions as
"piecemeal social engineering" and contrasts it with its opposite, holistic or
utopian engineering. The utopian social engineer attempts to remodel the whole of
society according to a given blueprint and rejects all hypotheses that do not
coincide with his plan. "By a rejection *a priori* of such hypotheses, the Utopian
approach violates the principles of scientific method," Popper maintains.[31]
Moreover, the utopian method, "wherever it has been tried, has led only to the use
of violence in place of reason."[32] The piecemeal social engineer, by contrast, may
have some cherished ideals, but he does not attempt to redesign society as a whole.

---

[28]Dürrenmatt, *Turmbau: Stoffe IV-IX* (Zürich: Diogenes, 1990), pp. 83-110.

[29]*Turmbau: Stoffe IV-IX*, p. 102.

[30]*Turmbau*, p. 86. He adds, however, that there are many physicists who hope to arrive
at this zero point. Their physical world-formula, he writes, would then also be a metaphysical
one (p. 86).

[31]Popper, "Piecemeal Social Engineering," in *Popper: Selections*, p. 311. Excerpted and
reprinted from Popper, *The Poverty of Historicism* (New York: Harper, 1977).

[32]Popper, *The Open Society and Its Enemies*, 1: 158.

"Whatever his ends, he tries to achieve them by small adjustments and re-adjustments which can be continually improved upon."[33] His approach is scientific in so far as it regards theories as "tentative hypotheses." He realizes that what is needed is not dogmatism, but "the adoption of a critical attitude, and the realization that not only trial but also error is necessary."[34]

In ideas of this kind, Dürrenmatt found a philosophical defense for what was no doubt an instinctive aversion to utopianism and a deep affinity for liberalism, a political outlook that may have been nurtured by Popper and others but that probably originated in Dürrenmatt's own experience as a young man growing up during the time of Hitler and Stalin. The central idea of Dürrenmatt's political thought is this: just as there can be no finality in scientific inquiry, there can be none in the political arena, where there will always be competition among a variety of viewpoints.[35] One of his main goals was to combat recurring attempts to end this competition in favor of an ultimate political solution, which he describes as the "romantic longing for a final system" (14: 188).[36] People instinctively regard the political process as the result of immutable "laws of nature" (28: 162) and the state as "something objective and independent of human beings" (29: 51), he maintains. In other words, people tend to reify the political process; they attempt, in the words of Peter Berger and Thomas Luckmann, to apprehend "the products of human activity *as if* they were something else than human products — such as facts of nature, results of cosmic laws, or manifestations of divine will."[37]

According to Dürrenmatt, political institutions must be regarded not as reified facticities but as hypotheses that can do no more than *approximate* the ideal. The state, he insists, is not "a mythological entity" but "a conscious fiction" set up by human beings in order to facilitate communal life (28: 38). As a product of human activity, every social or political order is by nature flawed; there is "no just social

[33]Popper, "Piecemeal Social Engineering," p. 309.

[34]Popper, "Piecemeal Social Engineering," pp. 314-15.

[35]The parallels between the method of science and the principles of liberalism have been pointed out by Ralf Dahrendorf: "The method of empirical science is strictly analogous to that of the political constitution of liberty. Knowledge by conflict corresponds to government by conflict." The basic principle of liberalism is "the institutional safeguarding of liberty by effective protection from the dogmatic establishment of one-sided positions." *Society and Democracy in Germany* (1967; New York: Norton, 1979), pp. 13, 150. See also Isaiah Berlin, "Two Concepts of Liberty," in *Liberalism and Its Critics*, ed. Michael J. Sandel (New York: New York University Press, 1984), pp. 15-36.

[36]It is for this reason that Dürrenmatt, like Popper, regards Plato as one of the enemies of the "open society." Based on abstractions and supposedly eternal verities, Plato's state, had it been erected, would have been "a hell of a state" ["eine Hölle von Staat"] (*Versuche*, p. 91).

[37]Peter Berger and Thomas Luckmann, *The Social Construction of Reality: A Treatise on the Sociology of Knowledge* (Garden City, New York: Doubleday, 1966), p. 82.

order" (27: 86). Like scientific conjectures, institutions ought to be viewed as tentative theories that are "always criticizable, testable...changeable" and "verifiable" (27: 147; 29: 187). Political thinking should be subjected to a Popperian "logic of science": "The logic of science leads through the elimination of error to objective knowledge, to progress" (27: 145-46). In this way, science can progress towards truth, and politics towards freedom and justice — truth, freedom, and justice functioning here in Popper's sense as "regulative ideas" in an inherently imperfect world where ultimate solutions cannot be found:

> 'Reasonableness,' understood as the search for truth, justice, and freedom, does not mean ignorance about what would be true, just, or free in the abstract. It means that we cannot proceed from truth, from justice, from freedom — from the ideal — but from the concrete. It means that in science we must approximate the truth and that in politics we must approximate justice and freedom... (27: 113).

An important role in this search for freedom and justice is played by language, conceived not as an instrument of metaphysical speculation but as discourse. Discourse is essential to politics, for it is only in the political realm, beyond the confines of religious and ideological dogmas, "in what is linguistically entirely imprecise and approximate; in the tedious testing of words in order to make oneself understood," that one can hope to find "a new meaning beyond language" (29: 109). The discovery of such a meaning would result in consensus. Dürrenmatt has little hope that this can ever be accomplished, but the possibility is there and it is occasionally articulated in his works, for example in his 1949 play *Romulus the Great* [*Romulus der Große*].

Romulus the Great is generally regarded as Dürrenmatt's first play in the comedic style that later became the hallmark of his work. I shall focus here particularly on the changes he made in the second version (1957) of the final act. In the first version of that act, Romulus outmaneuvered Odoaker and succeeded in bringing the Teutons under his power. Later, he voluntarily dissolved the empire, named Odoaker the new King of Italy, and retired. In the second version and those following, Romulus expects his death at the hands of Odoaker as atonement for his refusal to defend the guilt-laden Roman Empire, a policy that resulted in the death of many innocent people, including his own wife and daughter. Having heard of Romulus's peaceful and humane nature, however, Odoaker plans to submit himself and his people to the emperor's rule. This change is generally regarded as the "worst possible turn of events" for Romulus, for now he must continue to live with the knowledge of his own guilt. As he tells Odoaker: "Everything I have done has become absurd" (2: 109).[38] But this is only one aspect of the encounter between the two leaders. The interaction between Romulus and Odoaker also demonstrates the possibility of rational discourse and consensus, even between individuals with radically different conceptual frameworks.

[38]*Romulus the Great*, trans. Gerhard Nellhaus, in *Friedrich Dürrenmatt: Plays and Essays*, ed. Volker Sander, The German Library 89 (1964; New York: Continuum, 1982), p. 64. Further references will be indicated in the text by *Plays* and page number.

In this second version of the final act, Dürrenmatt altered his characterization of Odoaker in order to present him as a person capable of reason. In the first version, he was described as a "deeply barbaric, gigantic figure, clothed in a polar bear skin" (2: 135), a description that corresponded to the view Romulus was likely to have of him. In the second version, by contrast, Odoaker has "nothing barbarian about him." He enters the stage, "as if he were walking through a museum" (*Plays* 59; 2: 101). To Romulus's surprise, Odoaker appears as a civilized human being, and he chastises the emperor for his ethnocentrism: "Even a Teuton may be guided by reason, Emperor of Rome" (*Plays* 62; 2: 106). Odoaker's statement reflects a belief in what Karl Popper has called "the unity of human reason." It is based on the notion that "faith in reason is not only faith in my own reason, but also — and even more — in that of others." This implies that there is "a common language of reason" and that all human beings are united in their ability to use language "as an instrument of rational communication."[39] "Romulus, a moment ago we talked sensibly about chickens," Odoaker says. "Isn't it possible to talk just as sensibly about nations and people?" (*Plays* 62; 2: 106).

Because of this faith in reason and communication, Romulus and Odoaker are able to reach an agreement that, at least for a while, maintains peace and benefits both their peoples. Their discourse in the last act is an example of Habermasian communicative action. According to Habermas, the participants in communicative action are persuaded solely by the force of the better argument. Their discourse is oriented to truth (in the objective world), normative rightness (in the social world), and truthfulness (authenticity or sincerity).[40] The exchange between Romulus and Odoaker exemplifies these principles, even though the two leaders confront each other with two very different ideas of the future: Romulus expects his death and Odoaker plans to surrender to Romulus. They overcome their differences and arrive at consensus through a process of argument that is oriented toward finding the truth. When Romulus insists that Odoaker kill him, for example, Odoaker persuades him that his death could only be meaningful if the world were the way he had imagined it. Since the world is not this way, he concludes, Romulus's death would be pointless. Similarly, when Odoaker wants to murder his nephew Theoderich, Romulus dissuades him with the argument that such an act would in the long run be counterproductive, because a thousand new Theoderichs would rise up to take his nephew's place. As a result of this process of argumentation, each agrees to a course of action very different from the one he had originally planned: Romulus accepts his retirement instead of his death and Odoaker agrees to become King of Italy rather than Romulus's subject.

[39]Popper, *The Open Society and Its Enemies*, 2: 238-39. I do not mean to imply a direct influence of Popper on Dürrenmatt's thinking at this point. Dürrenmatt most likely did not read Popper until the late sixties. What is apparent already in 1957, however, is the affinity of some of their basic ideas.

[40]See my discussion of Habermas in the introduction.

Romulus and Odoaker both realize that this solution will be short-lived and that the implacable world will once again take its worst possible turn, this time in the form of Odoaker's nephew Theoderich, who will murder both of them. But their solution, which is the product of dialogue and mutual criticism, contains a political lesson that contrasts vividly with the absolutist and inevitably ruthless approach to political problems exemplified by Romulus's behavior in the first three acts. Romulus's approach earlier in the play was "unscientific," in Popper's sense, because it was dogmatic and holistic in intent. Convinced that his "hypothesis" about the guilty Roman Empire was true, he attempted to restructure or destroy the empire in accordance with his own absolute concept of justice. The suffering of individuals, represented by his daughter's fiancé Ämilian, who was tortured in Germanic captivity, was of no consequence. Romulus attempted to change the world through "pure" reason. Like F and Polyphem, he attempted to assume a god-like position of "pure observation." But, as Dürrenmatt insists, the attempt to solve political problems through a reliance on "pure" reason is inherently unreasonable: "The reasonable transformation of the world cannot be accomplished through pure thinking" (28: 39). In the final act of *Romulus the Great*, the locus of rationality shifts from the individual mind to communicative interaction, and the locus of political action moves from absolutism to democracy, whose "heart and final guarantee," as John Dewey has observed, is free communication.[41] The idea of communicative reason thus incorporates Dürrenmatt's epistemological as well as his political ideal. It contains the Popperian notion of knowledge as the product of critical discourse as well as the liberal notion of politics as a process of communication and ongoing criticism.

In this way, Dürrenmatt succeeds, despite his skepticism, in "saving" reason. A crucial role in his thinking is played by Popper's model of scientific method with its skeptical attitude toward claims to truth, its view of theories as tentative hypotheses, and its emphasis on critical discourse. For Dürrenmatt, as for Popper, "rational" means "critical." Indeed, the Popperian model of science attains such prestige in Dürrenmatt's thought that he does not hesitate to celebrate science as "value-free," declaring: "It is purely aesthetic, beautiful, beyond good and evil."[42] But such statements also lead his thinking into a contradiction. By claiming that science is value-free and beyond good and evil, Dürrenmatt transforms scientific method into a "safe" mode of inquiry removed from the vicissitudes that normally affect human undertakings. Adherence to the logic of science, he implies, would permit the inquirer to assume a position of "pure observation"; it would enable him or her to do precisely what Dürrenmatt so mercilessly condemns his fictional characters for attempting to do. Dürrenmatt thus makes

[41]John Dewey, "Creative Democracy — The Task Before Us," in Dewey, *The Later Works*, 17 vols., ed. Jo Ann Boydston (Carbondale, Illinois: Southern Illinois University Press, 1988), 14: 227.

[42]*Versuche*, p. 91.

himself vulnerable to charges of cryptic foundationalism and of scientism, which Habermas described as "science's belief in itself."[43]

Dürrenmatt would have undoubtedly rejected these charges, for he regarded a commitment to the rational, discursive principles embodied in scientific method as the only hope for a better world, even if this hope is, as *Romulus* shows, a slim one. Habermas's critique of science as an epistemological model has, however, found an echo in the writing of most of the other authors in this book. But before moving on to them, I shall contrast two very different attempts, one by Dürrenmatt and one by Rolf Hochhuth, to valorize science as the basis of political thinking and action. At center of these attempts stands the towering figure of Albert Einstein.

[43]Similar criticism has also been directed against Popper. See, for example, Habermas's contributions to *The Positivist Dispute in German Sociology*, trans. Glyn Adey and David Frisby (London: Heinemann, 1976); Thomas Kuhn, "Logic of Discovery or Psychology of Research," in *The Essential Tension: Selected Studies in Scientific Tradition and Change* (Chicago: University of Chicago Press, 1977), pp. 266-292; and Paul Feyerabend, *Against Method: Outline of an Anarchistic Theory of Knowledge* (London: NLB, 1975). See also the discussion of rationality and science in the introduction to this book.

2 Political Thinking in a Scientific Age: Hochhuth's *Judith* and Dürrenmatt's *Achterloo*

DESPITE THE DIFFERENCES in their aesthetic theories — one recalling the historical dramas of Schiller, the other the satirical comedies of Aristophanes — the outlooks of Rolf Hochhuth (b. 1931) and Friedrich Dürrenmatt show a number of striking similarities. One could point to their emphasis on the individual as a morally responsible agent, their rejection of the notion of any ultimate meaning in history, and their ongoing concern for justice and freedom.[1] One of the most important elements that unites them, however, is their vital commitment to what Ralf Dahrendorf has referred to as "public virtues,"[2] to issues of concern to men and women as members of society or the polity. One such issue is the nuclear arms race and the possibility of nuclear war — themes central to both *Judith* (1984) and *Achterloo* (1983). The responses of the characters in these plays to the nuclear threat — ranging from political assassination to political accommodation with the superpowers — suggest different modes of political thinking. The nature of this political thought, its epistemological foundations, and its consequences for political action in a scientific age will be the subject of this chapter.[3]

Hochhuth's and Dürrenmatt's interest in epistemological questions led them to scientific method as the field where questions of knowledge and truth are of pivotal

---

[1]For a comparison of the aesthetic theories and outlooks of Dürrenmatt and Hochhuth, see Margaret Ward, *Rolf Hochhuth*, Twayne's World Authors Series 463 (Boston: Twayne, 1977), pp. 118-25.

[2]Ralf Dahrendorf, *Society and Democracy in Germany* (1967; New York: Norton, 1979), p. 295.

[3]Both of these plays reflect the political situation in Europe in the mid-1980s. Some of the issues of concern here — the possibility of a nuclear confrontation between the superpowers, Germany's fate in any such war, Germany's re-unification and political orientation, the political situation in Poland — have shifted as a result of the unprecedented political changes in Europe since 1989. In this respect, the plays are not as topical as they were when they first appeared. This is also true of this essay, which was originally written in 1988. However, I believe the epistemological questions discussed here are still relevant for political thinking.

importance.[4] A common focus is the epistemology of Albert Einstein, discussed by Hochhuth in the foreword to his play *Guerillas* (1970) and by Dürrenmatt in his complex 1979 speech on the physicist.[5] The significance of Einstein's epistemology for both writers can be traced to his rejection of induction, the doctrine that theoretical knowledge derives from direct systematic observation of particular events. Instead, Einstein maintained that theories owe as much to intuition, imagination, and creative thinking as they do to empirical observation. "Intuition, not logic, is his destiny. More precisely, the logical adventure, not logical safeguards" (27: 167), Dürrenmatt comments.[6] The far-reaching implications of this insight for any theory of knowledge as well as for the notion of truth have been expounded by Karl Popper, who, as we have seen in the preceding chapter, stressed the importance of "creative intuition" in scientific discoveries. Popper's description of science as "the method of bold conjectures and ingenious and severe attempts to refute them" stresses the intuitive element in theory-making, the importance of criticism, and the hypothetical character of all knowledge.[7] Every

---

[4]Cf. Karl Popper: "The central problem of epistemology has always been and still is the problem of the growth of knowledge. *And the growth of knowledge can be studied best by studying the growth of scientific knowledge.*" Karl Popper, Preface to the English Edition 1958, *The Logic of Scientific Discovery*, trans. Karl Popper (New York: Basic Books, 1959), p. 15.

[5]See Hochhuth, *Guerillas: Tragödie in 5 Akten* [Guerillas: Tragedy in 5 Acts] (Reinbek: Rowohlt, 1970), pp. 8-9 and Dürrenmatt, "Albert Einstein," *Werkausgabe in dreißig Bänden* [Collected Works in Thirty Volumes] (Zürich: Diogenes, 1980), 27: 150-202. Future references to *Werkausgabe* will be indicated parenthetically in the text by volume and page number. Unless otherwise indicated, all translations are my own.

[6]"Die Intuition, nicht die Logik, ist sein Schicksal, genauer das logische Abenteuer, nicht die logische Absicherung." For Dürrenmatt, this is the most important element of Einstein's epistemology: "With that we have come to the most important dogma of Einstein's theory of knowledge. It is the conviction that sense experiences can be related only intuitively, not logically, to a conceptual system that is internally [in sich] logical but is, in an absolute sense [an sich], logically arbitrary" (27: 162). Likewise, Hochhuth quotes Einstein's assertion that knowledge arises "'only from the comparison of pre-existing thought [Vorbedachtem] with what is observed.'" *Guerillas*, p. 8.
See also Victor F. Lenzen: "The use of rational criteria for the construction of physical theories confirms Einstein's doctrine that concepts are free creations of the mind." According to Einstein, "an attempt to derive logically the concepts and laws of mechanics from the ultimate data of experience is doomed to failure. There is no inductive method that can lead to the fundamental concepts or principles. The truly creative principle of theoretical physics is mathematical construction." "Einstein's Theory of Knowledge," in *Albert Einstein: Philosopher-Scientist*, ed. Paul Arthur Schillp, 3rd ed., The Library of Living Philosophers 7 (La Salle, Illinois: Open Court, 1970), pp. 373-74.

[7]Karl R. Popper, *Objective Knowledge: An Evolutionary Approach* (Oxford: Carendon Press, 1972), p. 81. Italicized in the original.

scientific theory, he insists, is at most an "approximation to (absolute) truth."[8] The growth of knowledge results from hypotheses that are subjected to argument, criticism, and debate. What is important is the ongoing *search* for truth.

Ideas of this kind had a decisive influence not only on Dürrenmatt, but also on Hochhuth. In his 1981 speech "Aufblick zu Lessing" [Homage to Lessing], Hochhuth praised Lessing's refusal to regard any "truth" as final as well as his recommendation that even the search for truth be abandoned: the search could lead to the illusion that one has found it and thus to intolerance of opposing views.[9] Similarly, Dürrenmatt rejects all holistic, utopian thinking — thinking that presupposes knowledge of the truth — maintaining that politics should be based on an ongoing *search* for freedom and justice rather than on any attempt to restructure society as a whole in accordance with absolute moral precepts. Following Popper, he insists that, just as science can hope only for an approximation to (absolute) truth, politics can hope only for an approximation to (absolute) freedom and justice.[10]

This epistemological skepticism is based on the notion that human beings are likely to err and that viable solutions to problems can best be found through ongoing discussion with others. It suggests the need for an anti-authoritarian political system that encourages criticism so that opposing views can be heard. Such a political system would allow for argument, discussion, and debate to take place according to agreed-upon rules; it would be based on the premise that "the permanent conflict of parties is the only protection against the dogmatization of error."[11] In their essays and speeches, Hochhuth and Dürrenmatt have both committed themselves to these liberal principles. The end of opposition and conflict, according to Hochhuth, would mean the end of democracy, and he even opposes unity and consensus if they destroy "the electrically charged dialogue."[12] Dürrenmatt, too, stresses the necessity of regulated conflict when he refers to the state as a playing field on which political activity takes place according to "established rules" (29: 50). Freedom of thought is necessary, he insists, because only a political system based on criticism can guarantee that the state remain a human institution (28: 38-39).

In his prose fiction as well as in his plays, Dürrenmatt remains entirely consistent with these epistemological principles. One after the other, his plays

---

[8]Popper, *Objective Knowledge*, p. 126.

[9]Hochhuth, *Räuber-Rede. Drei deutsche Vorwürfe: Schiller/Lessing/Geschwister Scholl* [Brigands Speech. Three German Admonitions: Schiller, Lessing, the Scholls] (Reinbek: Rowohlt, 1982), p. 163-64.

[10]See chapter 1 above and *Werkausgabe*, 27: 113.

[11]Dahrendorf, p. 200.

[12]Hochhuth, *Krieg und Klassenkrieg: Studien* [War and Class War: Studies] (Reinbek: Rowohlt, 1971), p. 93.

demonstrate the folly of any actions based on presumed knowledge of the truth. The same cannot be said of Hochhuth, whose political activism and idealism sometimes lead him to assume positions that contradict his own stated epistemological premises. In the foreword to *Guerillas*, for example, he uses Einstein's epistemology as the point of departure for a revised view of historiography as well as of his dramatic theory, a change no doubt brought about by his turn, with *Guerillas*, to contemporary subject matter.[13] In both cases, Hochhuth focuses his attention on the element of intuition in Einstein's thinking. Thus, he maintains that the historian should not strive simply to give an account of the facts; he should use his intuition to seek out "historical constants" that can be used "for the projection of coming events, like a revolution" (*Guerillas* 10). Similarly, drama should not be content "to *reproduce* reality, which is of course always political; it must confront reality with the *projection* of a new one" (*Guerillas* 20). Dramatic characters should be "bearers of ideas" (20); as in Schiller, the play should strive to make visible "the deeper truth" (21). The "idea" represented by the protagonist should survive his or her tragic end and point to the possibility of a better world.[14] These notions introduce a utopian element into Hochhuth's dramaturgy that has important implications for his attitude toward truth and thus for his political thinking.[15] The consequences of this development are apparent not only in *Guerillas*, but also in *Die Hebamme* [The Midwife] (1971) and *Judith*.

The title figure of *Judith* is a young, idealistic American journalist who murders an American president committed to a massive arms buildup and a renewed production of chemical weapons. Judith plots the assassination of the president, who is clearly Ronald Reagan, together with her brother Arthur, a chemist by profession, who has been paralyzed as a result of contact with Agent Orange in Vietnam. Arthur is currently doing research on "a new, barely proven method of calculation that in certain — or better: in uncertain — cases would allow one to predict the attributes of certain molecules."[16] This reference to prediction

---

[13]For a more detailed discussion of these developments and their implications for Hochhuth's outlook and dramaturgy, see Margaret Ward, pp. 85-90.

[14]Cf. Walter Hinderer: "For [Hochhuth] a human being can outwardly be a victim of circumstances, but inwardly he or she demonstrates, despite everything, the principle of independence, as in dramas by Schiller....If [the positive figures] represent with their death the superiority of humane ideas, the outwardly victorious forces embody, as in Schiller, repulsive, irresponsible, corrupt, and unworthy behavior itself." "Hochhuth und Schiller — oder: Die Rettung des Menschen," *Rolf Hochhuth — Eingriff in die Zeitgeschichte: Essays zum Werk*, ed. Walter Hinck (Reinbek: Rowohlt, 1981), p. 73.

[15]Cf. Rainer Taeni, *Rolf Hochhuth*, Autorenbücher 5 (Munich: Beck, 1977), p. 25. Cf. also Manfred Durzak, "Amerikanische Mythologien. Zu Hochhuths Dramen '*Guerillas*' und '*Tod eines Jägers*,'" in *Eingriff in die Zeitgeschichte*, pp. 159-86.

[16]Hochhuth, *Judith: Trauerspiel* [Judith: A Tragedy] (Reinbek: Rowohlt, 1984), p. 174. Future references to the play will be indicated in the text by *J* and page number.

leads to the epistemological questions that are at the center of the play: Can present knowledge be used to predict future behavior? What constitutes "knowledge"? Can one predict the future actions of a human being? The answer given by Judith and Arthur to this last question seems to be "yes," for they are planning to murder the president even though there is no concrete evidence that he in fact intends to start a war. Arthur: "May one kill a person if one is convinced that he is about to wage war?" Judith: "Is one not *obligated* to do it?" ["*Muß* man es nicht?"] (*J* 186). Judith and Arthur base their convictions on the following observations: the president has unilaterally renewed the production of chemical weapons (cf. *J* 96, 101, 166); he allegedly believes that a nuclear war is winnable (*J* 161, 186) and that it can be confined to Europe (*J* 96); he apparently identifies our time with that described in the Apocalypse and is planning Armageddon (cf. *J* 105, 107, 181). Arthur also cites historical evidence. Based on the analogy of events leading to the First World War, he rejects the theory of deterrence, pointing out that arms races have historically always led to war (*J* 100).

Their friend Edward, a Jesuit priest, opposes these arguments on both logical and moral grounds. When Arthur asks him why they should not assassinate the president, Edward replies that they simply have no proof that he is about to start a war (*J* 161, 166). Because it is based on supposition and not knowledge, Edward condemns Arthur and Judith's plan as immoral: "Yes — because murder based on suspicion, murder as a preventative measure, is without doubt — without doubt! — the least justifiable" (*J* 168). Edward's opposition is based on a humanistic morality that emphasizes the fundamental worth and dignity of the individual. He is prepared to justify murder only when confronted with real evidence that such action is necessary: "Certainly, one must kill the person who is waging a world war" (*J* 156), he maintains. But no such evidence is presented by Judith and Arthur. In fact, there is evidence in the play that assassinations are pointless because the successors of assassinated political leaders are often worse. Regarding the murder of the Nazi commander of Minsk during World War II, for example, Judith herself observes: "The bloodhound Gottberg who succeeded him was incomparably worse!" (*J* 122).

Arthur and Judith are as unmoved by practical political considerations of this kind as they are by Edward's morality. They proceed instead from a position of moral absolutism. Their actions are fueled by a strong sense of injustice emanating from Arthur's bitterness over his paralysis and the indifference of the government to his plight. Despite the absence of evidence that the president is in fact planning a war, that, as her fiancé Gerald points out, the assassination will change nothing, and that indeed an even more dangerous leader may follow, Judith nevertheless believes that the murder is justified, not as a political act, but as a moral one that lends symbolic power to the "idea," "that it is *perverse*, against God, nature, and humanity, when the person who calmly [selbstverständlich] calculates the death of millions of people by poison gas dies peacefully in his bed" (*J* 204-05). Judith is prepared to commit murder in order to correct this "perverse" state of affairs. She is prepared to sacrifice a human life for the sake of an abstraction, the idea of justice.[17] After the assassination, she responds to Gerald's objections with the following rhetorical question: "Is an idea distorted by the fact that it only achieves symbolic force in reality?" (*J* 204). When such an idea entails murder, the answer to this question must certainly be "yes." Murder is not "symbolism"; it is murder. The taking of a human life ought to be based on solid evidence that such action is necessary in order to prevent a greater evil. Judith's statement betrays a belief in the existence of a realm of absolutes, of which real actions are merely pale reflections. Murder is justifiable in this view not for real political reasons, but because it is a symbol of a "higher" truth. Judith believes this truth can be known intuitively.[18] Rejecting critical discussion of the facts as the path to knowledge, she simply "knows" that she is right. And she clearly believes that those in possession of the truth are entitled to act on behalf of others. "But who...you are not the divine judge: who would have been permitted to make that decision?" (*J* 205), an exasperated Gerald asks her after the assassination.

Hochhuth takes pains to present balanced arguments for and against the assassination (as demonstrated by the exchange between Arthur and Edward in act III), and he claims in the "preamble" that he does not regard Judith and Arthur as "just" (*J* 8) and that he is not advocating violence. But in his notes following the play, he makes at least one authorial statement that can easily be seen as a defense of Judith's actions: "Politically great — are also morally great actions. For politics

---

[17]Judith's concept of justice is closely associated with the desire for vengeance, as the following passage indicates:

> When today Gandhi is constantly referred to, one suppresses the fact that even an *Indian* had to shoot. The governor, who had over 400 demonstrators shot at the massacre of Amritsar in 1919, was executed — it goes without saying — with a pistol, in London, twenty-one years after his atrocity, by the Indian Udham Singh. And it would be an *outrage*, if that had not happened! (*J* 181-82).

And regarding the assassination of the president, who is murdered with the same poison gas he has just ordered into production:

> Did it not finally have to become reality, instead of remaining forever a metaphor, that whoever lives by the sword shall die by the sword? (*J* 205).

Cf. also Manfred Durzak, who refers to "Hochhuth's Old Testament concept of justice." Durzak, "Ein Trauerspiel des Dramatikers Rolf Hochhuth. Anmerkungen zu seinem 'Judith'-Stück," *Hebbel-Jahrbuch 1987*, ed. Barbara Wellhausen, Wolfgang Damms, and Heinz Stolte (Heide: Westholsteinische Verlagsanstalt, 1987), p. 24.

[18]Thus, she believes that she and Arthur have the intuitive ability to "foresee" what the president will do: "Our cleaning woman does not have [access to that man over there]; nor does Bruce and nor do you — so you two are guiltless, *when the man does what we foresee that he will do*" ["*wenn der Mann macht, / was wir voraussehen, daß er's tut*"] (*J* 185-86; my italics). She becomes convinced of the truth of her decision to murder the president not through an analysis of the political consequences of the act, but intuitively as the result of "insights" gained in the second act from Teiresias, an epileptic "prophet" whose visions of the Apocalypse convince her that the Biblical prophecies refer to modern times. Reacting to his hallucinations, she is, as the stage direction tells us, "almost as paralyzed as the man tormented by his visions" (*J* 137).

is a supra-personal, public morality that is exercised on behalf of others" (*J* 227).[19] This statement, which seems to justify Judith's moral absolutism, implies a rejection of the playwright's own stated epistemological and political principles. His equation of politics with morality and his conviction that history is made by individuals[20] place him on a course that threatens to collide with the principles of criticism, argument, and debate that are fundamental to liberalism. Despite his praise for Lessing's critical approach and his rejection of all claims to final knowledge, Hochhuth now suggests that the critical method can be temporarily suspended by exceptional individuals who are convinced that they are in possession of the truth.[21]

It is this "knowledge" of the truth that propels not only Judith and Arthur, but also Senator Nicolson in *Guerillas* and Sophie in *Die Hebamme* to commit acts of such breathtaking folly. With a nuclear submarine and its missiles in his possession, Nicolson plans to stage a coup against the U.S. government. His goal: the establishment of an opposition working class party and thus of real democracy in America. Sophie leads the inhabitants of a slum dwelling to burn down their

[19]"Politisch große — sind auch moralisch große Dinge. Denn Politik ist ja die überpersönliche, die öffentliche und die zugunsten anderer geleistete Moral." For Manfred Durzak, this sentence is "the most frightful sentence of Hochhuth." He continues: "For centuries, this sentences has been used to justify the claims of the most diverse ideologies of power. Mountains of corpses have been piled up in the shadow of such a sentence, even in the most recent European history." "Ein Trauerspiel des Dramatikers Rolf Hochhuth. Anmerkungen zu seinem 'Judith'-Stück," 24. In his next sentence, Hochhuth implies that an individual with the necessary power and "insight" would be justified in using "brutality and cunning" against his opponents when he "sees" that they are not acting in the interest of the majority. He also suggests that such individuals ought to act in accordance with their "fore-sight" (*J* 227-28).

[20]"*Is there* history that is not made by individuals?" (*J* 230). His prime example is Hitler, who, he says, was alone responsible for the extermination of the Jews and the invasion of the Soviet Union, a fact that "increases" the guilt of those who did nothing to stop him (*J* 236).

[21]Hochhuth's ambivalent attitude toward the question of truth may also be responsible for the disagreement among critics regarding his political intentions. While some, such as Rainer Taeni, see Hochhuth as advocating revolution, others, such as Fritz Raddatz, regard him as a proponent of reform. Similarly, Ward refers to the fluctuations between optimism and pessimism in Hochhuth's *Weltanschauung*. Popper has shown that different approaches to political problems may be seen as reflections of different attitudes towards truth. The "optimistic" belief that "truth is manifest" underlies a holistic approach to problems and can thus be associated with a tendency to utopianism and revolution, while the "pessimistic" belief that the status of knowledge is tentative emphasizes the importance of caution and thus of piecemeal reform. See Rainer Taeni, *Rolf Hochhuth*, p. 24; Fritz J. Raddatz, "Der utopische Pessimist," *Rolf Hochhuth — Eingriff in die Zeitgeschichte*, p. 51; Margaret Ward, p. 87; and Karl Popper, "On the Sources of Knowledge and Ignorance," *Conjectures and Refutations: The Growth of Scientific Knowledge* (1962; New York: Harper, 1965), pp. 3-30. On the connections between epistemology and political thinking see also Bertrand Russell, "Philosophy and Politics," *Unpopular Essays* (New York: Simon and Schuster, 1950), pp. 1-20.

homes and occupy a new army barracks.[22] Like Judith and Arthur, these characters are motivated by a sense of outrage at the discrepancy between the inequities and inevitable corruption of the real world and their own ideal of justice. This results in an impatience with the give-and-take of the political process, which is abandoned in favor of unconventional and frequently violent methods that are motivated by a desire for quick and unambiguous solutions to problems. Although Hochhuth does not explicitly endorse the actions of these characters, he has made a number of statements, such as the one quoted above, that seem to be rooted in the same absolutist mentality that animates them. Other examples are his well-intentioned but impractical demand that society's wealth be divided "again and again in proportion to the number of inhabitants" and his contention that democracy can exist only "where the tax payer himself determines the *application* of every portion of his taxes that does not benefit the common good."[23] Rather than accept the notions of conflict and compromise as an inevitable part of the political process, these assertions reflect what Dahrendorf has referred to as a "nostalgia for synthesis," a longing for "substantively final solutions, for justice itself, which must yet remain uncertain."[24] With such statements, Hochhuth strays from the realm of practical politics to that of romantic utopianism.

Dürrenmatt was always wary of the political implications of this kind of thinking. The type of character Hochhuth selects as his "tragic" heroes, the absolutist bearers of his utopian ideas, most often exemplifies in Dürrenmatt's plays the epitome of foolishness, a fact that also led him to reject unequivocally the drama of Schiller: "Historical drama with idealized human beings, as in Schiller, does not interest me."[25] Dürrenmatt insists that one must proceed not from the absolute, the ideal, but from the concrete, and that one must always look first to the practical consequences of an idea in the real world:

> By abolishing metaphysics, one concedes that justice or world revolution are not metaphysical. Justice becomes a rule among human beings and the world revolution becomes a utopia, a land of nowhere. This linguistic housecleaning is

[22]Cf. Margaret Ward, who notes that Nicolson "tends to think in absolutes" and that he "moves dangerously close to a position which Hochhuth had so eloquently argued against in *Soldiers* — that any end justifies the means." Ward, p. 94. In a review of *Die Hebamme*, Helmut Karasek "accused Hochhuth of having fascist tendencies, on the grounds that his central tenet, which places individual initiative above authority, is a step in the direction of the 'call for a strong man.'" Cited by Ward, p. 108.

[23]Hochhuth, *Die Hebamme: Komödie. Erzählungen. Gedichte. Essays* [The Midwife: A Comedy. Stories. Poems. Essays]. Die Bücher der Neunzehn 203 (Reinbek: Rowohlt, 1971), pp. 113, 114.

[24]Dahrendorf, *Society and Democracy in Germany*, pp. 178, 184.

[25]Friedrich Dürrenmatt and Charlotte Kerr, *Rollenspiele: Protokoll einer fiktiven Inszenierung und Achterloo III* [Role-Plays: Record of a Fictitious Production and Achterloo III] (Zürich: Diogenes, 1986), p. 129.

beneficial, particularly today... Freedom, justice, ideas, metaphysical principles, to what end, if no one is there any more who can set them up or to whom that can be applied? Ideas are guiding principles established by human beings. As such I can accept them.[26]

The opposition between this kind of thinking and the absolutism exemplified by Judith is the subject of Dürrenmatt's *Achterloo*.

Achterloo is actually a play-within-a-play put on by the inmates of a mental asylum, each patient assuming the role of an historical personage.[27] The action of the play is based on the events in Poland that led to the imposition of martial law in 1981. The absolutists are represented by inmates portraying contemporary versions of Cardinal Richelieu and Robespierre. Dürrenmatt states that the aged Robespierre, now the Communist Party ideologist, can be played by a girl (*A* 48). He spends his brief time on stage spouting ideological platitudes, blissfully unaware of any potentially contradictory facts. Robespierre symbolizes the impotence of abstract ideological thinking when confronted with reality: he collapses on stage after his first sexual experience ever. He is described as an asexual child because his ideology has nothing to do with life. It is only "true" as an abstraction; when confronted with real problems, it falls apart. Richelieu's attitude makes it clear that the only way to secure such absolutist thinking is through oppression. In order to defend their ideologies against religious and

---

[26]*Rollenspiele*, pp. 114-15. Dürrenmatt's position recalls the pragmatism of William James:

> Metaphysics has usually followed a very primitive kind of quest. You know how men have always hankered after unlawful magic, and you know what a great part in magic *words* have always played....You can rest when you have them. You are at the end of your metaphysical quest.
>
> But if you follow the pragmatic method, you cannot look on any such words as closing your quest. You must bring out of each word its practical cash-value, set it at work within the stream of your experience. It appears less as a solution, then, than as a program for more work, and more particularly as an indication of the ways in which existing realities may be *changed*.

James, *Writings 1902-1910*, ed. Bruce Kuklick (New York: Library of America, 1987), p. 509.

[27]There are two printed versions of the play: *Achterloo: Eine Komödie in zwei Akten* [Achterloo: A Comedy in Two Acts] (Zürich: Diogenes, 1983) and *Achterloo III: Ein Rollenspiel* [Achterloo III: A Role-Play] (1986) (in Dürrenmatt and Kerr, *Rollenspiele*). (A second version of the play was not printed.) As the subtitle implies, there is a much greater emphasis in the 1986 version on the notion of role-playing. In addition to their roles as patients, most characters are now also given a "Stage Role" and a "Delusional Role"; in order to explain and justify these roles, long monologues have been inserted into the play. Dürrenmatt seems more interested here in the aesthetic, theatrical, and psychological implications of this role-playing than in the play's political dimension. As a consequence, the impact of the play as a political statement, and as a commentary on current events, is diminished. For these reasons, my discussion will focus on the 1983 version. Future references to the play will be taken from this version and indicated parenthetically in the text by *A* followed by page number.

political "heretics," Richelieu proposes that the two rival contenders for the truth, the Church and the Party, form a Catholic-Marxist union. This union would provide the solution to both their problems: an escape-proof cage for mankind (*A* 36-37).

In the second act, Richelieu comes to recognize the folly and inhumanity of this absolutist mentality. He realizes now that the attempt to force imperfect human beings to conform to "perfect" ideologies can only lead to "hell on earth" (*A* 87). Richelieu's change of heart results from his epistemological insight into the real nature of these ideologies and their relation to truth. He understands now that, although such logical constructs may be true when measured against themselves [*in sich*], it does not follow that they are also true absolutely [*an sich*]. Logical constructs have no claim to (absolute) truth: "Some scholar, who thought about space and time, once wrote: Insofar as the axioms of mathematics refer to reality, they are not certain; and insofar as they are certain, they do not refer to reality" (*A* 85). The scholar referred to is Albert Einstein, who made this observation in his lecture "Geometrie und Erfahrung" [Geometry and Experience].[28] Einstein's comment emphasizes once again the tentative, hypothetical nature of all theories and thus of all claims to truth. Richelieu is quick to draw the practical consequences from this epistemological fact:

> What the unknown scholar wrote also applies to theology and to ideology: insofar as the propositions of theology and of ideology refer to human beings, they are not certain; and insofar as they are certain, they do not refer to human beings. Theology and ideology are only true in a space devoid of human beings (*A* 86).

Richelieu's statement exposes as epistemologically untenable all attempts to base one's actions on knowledge of the truth and, founded on this supposed knowledge, to force human beings to conform to a preconceived ideological system.[29] It implies a rejection of absolutism in favor of an approach that looks upon ideas, in Dürrenmatt's words, "as guiding principles established by human beings" and that asks about their practical consequences in the real world rather than their absolute truth value.

The political consequences of this kind of thinking are demonstrated by Napoleon, the prime minister in Dürrenmatt's play-within-a-play, who must deftly maneuver his country between the two superpowers in order to avoid war and a

[28]Albert Einstein, "Geometrie und Erfahrung," in Einstein, *Mein Weltbild*, ed. Carl Seelig (Berlin: Ullstein, 1989), pp. 119-20. Also quoted by Dürrenmatt in *Werkausgabe* 27: 180. Commenting elsewhere on this statement by Einstein, Dürrenmatt notes that mathematical models are certain only internally [*in sich*], that is, when measured against themselves, but that they are not certain in an absolute sense [*an sich*], that is, when measured against reality (29: 171).

[29]Cf. Dürrenmatt: "We return again and again to the same starting point: because every human being is an individual, he or she is a mystery, and because each is a mystery, he or she cannot be explained in terms of a system. A system knows no mysteries; it is without mysteries" (14: 267).

possible nuclear confrontation. In order to prevent an invasion, Napoleon betrays Jan Hus, the leader of the independent trade union, with whose political goals he sympathizes, and has him arrested. For this, he is regarded as a traitor by the patriotic Marion: "You have betrayed us, instead of fighting" (*A* 106). When Marion reminds him of the victories of the historical Napoleon, he replies that such victories are a thing of the past: "All too easily today do victories plunge peoples into misfortune. Woe to the victors" (*A* 108). Napoleon believes that his actions represent "the only solution" (*A* 113), for if he had supported the trade union, the Soviet Union would have invaded his country. This would have necessitated a response from the other superpower that might have led to war. Napoleon chooses treason over annihilation: "I am the lesser evil that prevents the grand pose: the heroic struggle of a people with millions of dead" (*A* 108).

The difference between this pragmatic outlook and the absolutism presented in Hochhuth's play can be seen in the way the two playwrights deal with the myth of Judith, the Biblical patriot who saved the Hebrews from foreign domination by murdering the Assyrian general Holofernes. Hochhuth's play is clearly intended as a reference to the Biblical story, from which he quotes at the beginning of the printed version of the text (*J* 13) and which is discussed by Judith and Arthur in the first act (*J* 84-85; 106). There are three Judith figures in his drama: Jelena, the Russian Judith (presented in the prologue and again in the second act) who murdered the Nazi commander of the city of Minsk during World War II; the "Judith of Nicaragua," Nora Astorga, who murdered a CIA informer (see *J* 146-48); and finally the American Judith, who murders the U.S. president. Hochhuth's goal is to visualize the unifying principle — or "historical constant" — common to the four assassinations: the viability of assassination as a political tool of the otherwise impotent masses against the all-powerful few. As Judith puts it: "Perhaps, Jelena, this is the deepest significance of historical assassinations: to struggle against the impotence of the many under the omnipotence of the few?" (*J* 127; see also 208). In the second act, during her interview with Jelena, Judith explicitly draws a parallel between the actions of the Russian and the Biblical Judiths (*J* 119-20), a parallel that — as the stage direction suggests — she extends also to herself: "The American is very excited, for Jelena has liberated the idea that has preoccupied Judith for several months and united it with the main artery of historical tradition" (*J* 128). In order to make the connection between Jelena and Judith — and their victims — clear, Hochhuth suggests that the Russian Judith of the prologue and the American Judith be played by the same actress (*J* 54). In the third act, a parallel is also drawn between the Biblical and the Nicaraguan Judith. When seen against the backdrop of the Biblical story, each of these assassinations appears as a variation of the mythical struggle between Judith and Holofernes, between freedom and oppression, good and evil.

Hochhuth's strategy resembles a procedure that William James has referred to as "vicious abstractionism," the process of "singling out some salient or important feature" in a concrete situation and "reducing the originally rich phenomenon to the naked suggestions of that name abstractly taken, treating it as a case of 'nothing but' that concept."[30] Hochhuth presents each of the assassinations discussed in the play as variations of a mythical and therefore timeless heroic act. Despite his insistence that one must begin with historical facts, his procedure in *Judith* eschews the examination of historical details in favor of an approach that suggests that the truth or *essence* of an historical event can be known intuitively.[31] This essence is presented as a universally and eternally valid "historical constant." It is precisely this kind of thinking, with its underlying preoccupation with abstractions, absolutes, and essences, that Dürrenmatt always opposed. The purpose of *Romulus the Great*, for example, with its two competing notions of justice, represented by Romulus and Ämilian, is not to discover the *essence* of justice, but to determine the consequences of the two concepts — as James might say, their "practical cash-value" — in society. Dürrenmatt's approach is the application even to questions of morality of the need to *search* for the truth. It implies that, just as there is no criterion of absolute truth, so too is there no criterion of absolute rightness. Values evolve as the result of constant criticism, argument, and communication among men and women who are committed to solving problems.[32]

Dürrenmatt's treatment of the Judith myth in *Achterloo* reflects this need to search continuously for new standards, to rethink old attitudes. Convinced that she has become a patriotic Judith, Marion kills Napoleon: "I have killed him. I have killed Holofernes" (*A* 117). Marion's action is animated by the same heroic thinking that characterized Hochhuth's Judith, but Dürrenmatt clearly shows this kind of thinking to be hopelessly anachronistic in a nuclear age: Marion murders the one man who was capable of saving his country from war and possible destruc-

---

[30]James, *Writings*, p. 951.

[31]For a discussion of the notions of intuitive understanding of socio-historical events, of inference by analogy from one historical period to another, and of essentialism, see Karl Popper, *The Poverty of Historicism*, 3rd ed. (1961; New York: Harper, 1964), pp. 19-24 and 26-34.

[32]Cf. Karl Popper, who notes that "in a sense we *create* our standards by proposing, discussing, and adopting them." He continues that

we may take the idea of absolute truth — of correspondence to the facts — as a kind of model for the realm of standards, in order to make it clear to ourselves that, just as we may *seek* for absolutely true propositions in the realm of facts or at least for propositions which come nearer to the truth, so we may *seek* for absolutely right or valid proposals in the realm of standards — or at least for better, or more valid, proposals.

However, it would be a mistake...to extend this attitude beyond the *seeking* to the *finding*. For though we should seek for absolutely right or valid proposals, we should never persuade ourselves that we have definitely found them; for clearly, there cannot be a *criterion of absolute rightness* — even less than a criterion of absolute truth."

Karl Popper, "Facts, Standards, and Truth: A Further Criticism of Relativism," *The Open Society and Its Enemies*, 5th ed., 2 vols. (Princeton: Princeton University Press, 1966), 2: 385-86.

tion. Napoleon tried to convince Marion that this kind of thinking is meaningless in the modern age: "When Judith killed Holofernes, her country was liberated. If you kill me, the absurdity of our bondage will only increase" (*A* 110). Napoleon portrays the idealism of Marion — and by extension of Hochhuth's Judith — as an outdated pose that is only "true," as Richelieu said, "in a space devoid of human beings." Where Hochhuth attempts to depict such ideas as universally valid, Dürrenmatt regards them as hypotheses that need to be constantly tested against changing political and historical realities. In a nuclear age, Dürrenmatt implies, the need for such testing and rethinking is more urgent than ever.

Judith and *Achterloo* both reflect their authors' concern for the urgent political issues of the mid-1980s: the nuclear arms race, the possibility of nuclear war and its consequences for Europe, and the question of neutrality. For Hochhuth, who was active in the peace movement, these issues — particularly the stockpiling of weapons on German soil and the question of German neutrality (cf. *J* 103-04; 177-78) — were of vital importance. In the third act of *Judith*, the (American) professor refers to the "unbelievably stupid Germans who stockpile our poison like beer" (*J* 178). The play was Hochhuth's protest against these threatening developments.[33] Judith's assassination of the president was an act of desperation reflecting a widespread *Angst* about the nuclear arms race and the likely fate of Germany in any confrontation between the superpowers.[34] Hochhuth's solution to these problems seemed to be neutrality (cf. *J* 252-54). But just as Judith's assassination of the president reflected a romantic desire for "synthesis," for justice itself, Hochhuth's call for neutrality resembled more a utopian longing for an idyll removed from history than a realistic political solution. At the close of his "Räuber-Rede" [Brigands Speech, a reference to Schiller's play] in 1982, he called on German youth to transform Germany into an island of freedom ever safe from war:

> That's how it is today: no map, no emigration can show us the blessed [selig] land where we would be free from war. Here in this land...only here can this island of peace be created, through the radicalism of our youth, our '*brigands*' (p. 103).

[33]According to Jürgen Habermas, the anti-nuclear and peace movements were two "key phases" in a much broader protest movement against developments "that visibly attack the *organic foundations of the life-world.*" Jürgen Habermas, "New Social Movements," *Telos* 49 (fall 1981): 34-5. The question of the peace movement and its role in the contemporary German scene is a complex one. See also Joachim Hirsch, "The West German Peace Movement," trans. David Berger, *Telos* 51 (spring 1982): 135-41; Russell Berman, "Opposition to Rearmament and West German Culture," *Telos* 51 (spring 1982): 141-48; and Seyla Benhabib, "The West German Peace Movement and Its Critics," *Telos* 51 (spring 1982): 148-58.

[34]Cf. Walter Laqueur, *Germany Today: A Personal Report* (Boston: Little, Brown, 1985), pp. 5-16.

Is this political thinking or utopian dreaming?[35]

Judith is a political play in that it deals with topical issues and contributes to consciousness-raising, but despite its high-mindedness it suggests no realistic political alternatives. *Achterloo* is political in a deeper and more far-reaching sense, for it strives to get to the root of the matter: our thinking. It demonstrates the inadequacy of traditional modes of political thought and suggests the necessity of re-examining our political thinking as the first step toward the discovery of *real* solutions to political problems. Dürrenmatt was always convinced that thinking changes the world: "Not he who wants to change the world changes it with time; but he who interprets it" (28: 167). *Achterloo* is one of his last contributions to this rethinking process as the necessary prerequisite for any political change.

Dürrenmatt is the only author in this book for whom science and scientific rationality continued to provide a model for thought and action. As the locus of mutual criticism and of free and open discussion, science, as Dürrenmatt apprehends it, sets a *moral example* for the rest of society, particularly for politics: it exemplifies the principles of communication, argument, and mutual criticism that form the basis of liberalism.[36] Dürrenmatt believed that literature should contribute to this critical discourse. By criticizing established modes of thought, a play such as *Achterloo* furthers the establishment of *new public meanings*. In this way, it contributes to the vitality of the *public sphere* and thus of the democratic process. For the authors discussed in the following chapters, science has lost this

---

[35]Cf. Walter Laqueur, who regarded calls for German neutrality as misguided:
The era of a German *Sonderweg* pursued through military means is past and will not recur. But the Pied Piper can appear in many disguises and he can play more than one tune; a *Sonderweg* can also be followed by means other than war and this dream has not vanished: why make Germany the main battlefield of the future if it could attain safety through neutrality between West and East? It is a delusion, but those familiar with the attraction which myths have exerted in the history of nations — and German history is as good an example as any — will not dismiss the possibility that a myth of this kind may attract even more followers than it has at present." *Germany Today*, p. 174.
With the re-unification of Germany in 1990, the decision that the new Germany will, with the blessing of the USSR, be a member of NATO, and the apparent end of Communism in the Soviet Union, the question of German neutrality has lost its urgency. The new question, of course, is what role a new and powerful Germany will play in Europe. Whether the myth of a romantic *Sonderweg* for Germany influences the answer Germans give to this question remains to be seen.

[36]See also Richard Rorty: "We should think of the institutions and practices which make up various scientific communities as providing suggestions about the way in which the rest of culture might organize itself." These institutions "give concreteness and detail to the idea of 'unforced agreement.' Reference to such institutions fleshes out the idea of 'a free and open encounter' — the sort of encounter in which truth cannot fail to win." "Science as Solidarity," in *The Rhetoric of the Human Sciences: Language and Argument in Scholarship and Public Affairs*, eds. John S. Nelson, Allan Megill, and Donald N. McCloskey (Madison: University of Wisconsin Press, 1987), p. 46.

exemplary status. Most frequently, it is regarded not as a model of critical discourse but as a form of exploitation and domination that has obliterated the possibility of new public meanings. As a result, these writers turn inward and embark on a search for private meanings to replace the disintegration of the public sphere.

3 The Crisis of Scientific Knowledge and the End of the Subject: Thomas Bernhard

SCIENTIFIC EPISTEMOLOGIES HAVE TRADITIONALLY posited the separation of subject and object. In positivist theories, for example, "the knowing subject is set against an assumed independent natural reality, and the subject is supposed to 'reflect' the world in knowledge, either by means of images in the mind or by propositions in language that are in one-to-one correspondence with the facts."[1] The decline of this idea has had far-reaching consequences for both science and philosophy. According to Stanley Aronowitz:

> The crisis in science has occurred because of the challenge posed by Heisenberg and others to its positivist assumptions, particularly the notion that the relation of the observer to the observed is unproblematic. When Heisenberg reduced to mathematical language the simple notion that what is observed depends on the apparatus of observation, that is, depends on experiment, the scientificity of science was thrown into question.

Heisenberg suggested that the object is constituted by the mode of inquiry, with the result that, in Aronowitz's words, "scientific theory describes the relation of humans to the object of knowledge, not the objects themselves, taken at a distance."[2] This development contributed to the demise of the notion that the mind accurately reflects or represents knowledge. Richard Rorty has described this idea, which has a long history in philosophy, as the Mirror of Nature, and Joseph Margolis has referred to it similarly as the "transparency thesis."[3] The rejection

---

[1] Michael A. Arbib and Mary B. Hesse, *The Construction of Reality* (Cambridge: Cambridge University Press, 1986), p. 159.

[2] Aronowitz, *Science as Power: Discourse and Ideology in Modern Society* (Minneapolis: University of Minnesota Press, 1988), pp. 330-31.

[3] The transparency thesis refers to "all doctrines...by which one holds that there is a determinate match or adequation between the cognizable properties of the real world and the cognizing powers of the human mind...the world, or key parts of it, are in this sense cognitively transparent to the mind." Joseph Margolis, *Pragmatism without Foundations: Reconciling Realism and Relativism* (Oxford: Basil Blackwell, 1986), p. xvi. Richard Rorty

of the transparency thesis meant the end of certainty. It lent credence to the view that subject and object, knower and known, are one.

Although science does not occupy the same prominent position in the work of Thomas Bernhard (1931-1989) as it did in that of Dürrenmatt, his novels document a continuing preoccupation with the traditional epistemological assumptions of scientific rationality. The dichotomy of subject and object is reflected in virtually every novel in the relationship between an observer and an observed. Faithful adherents of the transparency thesis, some of Bernhard's observers even claim that intensive and concentrated observation can lead to insight into the very essence of a thing. The young narrator of *Gargoyles* [*Verstörung*], for example, claims to have experienced moments when he felt "empowered" to "see right through the whole of creation" (*G* 40-41; *V* 40).[4] Similarly, the more that Murau, the narrator of *Auslöschung: Ein Zerfall* [Obliteration: A Disintegration], observes the photographs of his family, the more he becomes convinced that he is able to see through the camera's distortions and perceive "the truth and the reality" of the depicted figures (*A* 30). The notion of transparency is clearly illustrated in Murau's equation of *looking at* [*anschauen*] with *looking through* [*durchschauen*], a technique he claims to have applied successfully to his parents at a very early age:

> At first I looked at them *in disbelief*, as they say; then I stared at them, and finally one day I *looked through* them. They never forgave me that; they could never forgive that. I had looked through them, as they say, and subjected them to an incorruptible evaluation that could not please them. To put it harshly, in giving birth to me they had given birth to their own dissector and subverter (*A* 152).

has also emphasized the importance of such "perceptual metaphors." See Rorty, *Philosophy and the Mirror of Nature* (Princeton: Princeton University Press, 1979), esp. pp. 155-64.

[4]References to the novels will be indicated parenthetically in the text as follows. Unless otherwise indicated, all translations are my own.

F   = *Frost* (1963; Frankfurt: Insel/Suhrkamp, 1972).
V   = *Verstörung* (Frankfurt: Insel/Suhrkamp, 1967).
G   = *Gargoyles* [*Verstörung*], trans. Richard and Clara Winston (New York: Knopf, 1970; Chicago: University of Chicago Press, 1986).
Ka = *Das Kalkwerk* (Frankfurt: Suhrkamp, 1970).
L   = *The Lime Works*, trans. Sophie Wilkins (New York: Knopf, 1973; Chicago: University of Chicago Press, 1986.
Ko = *Korrektur* (Frankfurt: Suhrkamp, 1975).
C   = *Correction*, trans. Sophie Wilkins (New York: Knopf, 1979).
B   = *Beton* (Frankfurt: Suhrkamp, 1982).
Co = *Concrete*, trans. David McLintock (New York: Knopf, 1984).
U   = *Der Untergeher* (Frankfurt: Suhrkamp, 1983).
L   = *The Loser*, trans. Jack Dawson (New York: Knopf, 1991).
H   = *Holzfällen: Eine Erregung* (Frankfurt: Suhrkamp, 1984).
W   = *Woodcutters*, trans. David McLintock (New York: Knopf, 1987).
AM = *Alte Meister: Komödie* (Frankfurt: Suhrkamp, 1985).
OM = *Old Masters: A Comedy*, trans. Ewald Osers (London: Quartett, 1989).
A   = *Auslöschung: Ein Zerfall* (Frankfurt: Suhrkamp, 1986).

Similarly, in *Correction* [*Korrektur*] Roithamer claims that his "art of observation" and "science of observation" have enabled him to "grasp" his sister's "nature" and represent it in a cone-shaped residence, which he claims "corresponds" to her "perfectly" (*C* 158-59; *Ko* 214-217). All of these characters attempt to found their claims to knowledge on intensive and concentrated observation; they all suggest that the mind is a mirror that accurately reflects the truth about a transparently knowable world, an idea graphically demonstrated by Roithamer's belief that the perceived essence of his sister can be represented in a physical structure and that his sister, his perception of her, and the cone all "correspond."[5]

It is, however, immediately apparent to the reader, and at times to the protagonist himself, that this observation is self-referential: the "truth" the protagonist claims to perceive is in fact a projection of his own mind. Subject and object, knower and known, the novels imply, are identical. The collapse of the notion of a transparently knowable world coincides with the end of the autonomous subject. Like Dürrenmatt, Bernhard rejects the notion that it is possible to assume a position of "pure observation." But unlike Dürrenmatt, he does not retain a faith in the possibility of acquiring objective knowledge through discourse and rational criticism. Confronted with their cognitive impotence, Bernhard's protagonists withdraw into monologic, subjective universes. Communicative interaction, like autonomy, falls victim to Bernhard's unrelenting epistemological skepticism.

The disintegration of the knowing subject begins already in Bernhard's first novel, *Frost* (1963). Although the young medical student attempts to convince the surgeon in his first letter reporting on the latter's brother that he has maintained "the prescribed line of clear, calculating reason" (*F* 296), that is, that he has upheld the position of objective observer, he admits in his notes of the twenty-fifth day "that the painter has taken possession of me....Me, his simple, weak observer." With the destruction of his privileged position as knowing subject, he loses all sense of identity: "I am no longer myself. No, no, I am no longer myself, I thought" (*F* 281).[6] Like the medical student, the young narrator of *Gargoyles* (1967) is also initially confident of his perceptive faculties. Just as he professed to be able to "see through" creation, he also regards family difficulties, which he has dealt with in a recent letter to his father, as transparent, analyzable, and solvable. As a result of his "analysis," which is based on "observations" he has made over many years and is supported by "evidence," he claims to have been able to sketch "a picture of us that could be considered truthful [wahr] from all...sides" (*G* 18-

---

[5]In a variation on this idea, hearing is substituted for seeing in *The Lime Works* [*Das Kalkwerk*]. Konrad claims to be able to hear sounds inaudible to others, such as "the incessant motion of the air" or "the movements in the deeps, the sounds of movements in the depths [of the water]" (*L* 75; *Ka* 70).

[6]For a more detailed analysis of perception and observation in *Frost* see Bernd Seydel, *Die Vernunft der Winterkälte: Gleichgültigkeit als Equilibrismus im Werk Thomas Bernhards*, Epistemata. Würzburger Wissenschaftliche Schriften. Reihe Literaturwissenschaft 22 (Würzburg: Königshausen und Neumann, 1986), esp. pp. 60-84.

19; *V* 21-22). This notion of a transparent and knowable world is challenged by the scenes of unmotivated murder, cruelty, and increasing mental and physical degeneracy that enfold before him as he accompanies his father on his medical rounds. Although the effect of this tour on the student is not made explicit in the novel, it is clear to the reader that any number of observations, investigations, and proofs will not produce a true picture of this world. Both students attempt to counter these threats to their cognitive autonomy by engaging in an exercise designed to re-establish the subject/object dichotomy. In *Frost*, the medical student undertakes a lengthy and detailed description of his room in which everything is made to appear connected with everything else: "From every object, from everything one can derive everything else. Isn't that a proof for everything?" (*F* 119). This attempt to "prove" that the world is after all cognitively transparent to the mind is as unsuccessful as that undertaken by his counterpart in *Gargoyles*, who attempts, somewhat feebly, to escape a feeling of depression and bewilderment in the darkness of the ravine by concentrating upon "a precise vision of [his] dormitory room" (*G* 71; *V* 68).

The students' nostalgia for precise observation, clarity, and connectedness is demolished by the prince, who contends in his long monologue in *Gargoyles* that the world is not cognitively transparent to the mind but opaque. He speaks of the mind's "numbing incapacity for perception, incapacity for observation, incapacity for receptivity" (*G* 123; *V* 116). The world is drenched in our own imagination, in what we have projected into it. "The only force that exists...is the force of imagination. Everything is imagined" (*G* 174; *V* 162). We are trapped within our own Kuhnian paradigms, our own "imaginary consciousness" (*G* 181; *V* 169), from which there is no escape. The prince's epistemology seems to derive from a radical interpretation of Kant, whom he describes as the last philosopher to let any "fresh air" into the museum of philosophy (*G* 176; *V* 164). Although he stressed the role played by the mind in organizing sensory data, Kant also seemed convinced that the mind merely registered the order of an independently existing reality and that the categories according to which we perceive the world of appearances were universal.[7] The prince not only inflates the role of "the force of imagination" in this process, he also suggests that each individual has his own set of categories that determine his perception. The result is that every individual is trapped within his own conceptual system: "Everything is always in all heads. Only in all heads. There is nothing outside of heads" (*G* 147-48; *V* 139). The world is not transparent; it is a projection of the individual mind.

---

[7] See Patrick Gardiner, "German Philosophy and the Rise of Relativism," *The Monist* 64 (1981): 145-46 and Jack W. Meiland and Michael Krausz, "Introduction," *Relativism: Cognitive and Moral* (Notre Dame, Indiana: Notre Dame U Press, 1982), p. 7. As the authors point out, the emphasis by later thinkers on the mind's activity in ordering experience became the basis for relativism. The relevance of Kant's thinking for Bernhard has also been noted by Hartmut Reinhardt, "Das kranke Subjekt. Überlegungen zur monologischen Reduktion bei Thomas Bernhard," *Germanisch-romanische Monatshefte* NS 26 (1976): 334-56.

In repudiating the notion of a cognitively transparent world, the prince is rejecting the epistemology upon which not only the two students but most of Bernhard's protagonists attempt, at least initially, to found their autonomy. Although many of his protagonists continue to assert their privileged positions as observing and knowing subjects, none of them is able to maintain this stance. They are forced to retreat into themselves, in effect drawing the logical consequence of the prince's epistemology, and to attempt to define their identities in terms of their own subjective universes. This process is the subject of *Correction* and *Auslöschung*.

In *Correction* (1975), the epistemological questions are dealt with on two levels: in the relationship between the narrator and Roithamer's papers and between Roithamer and his two major projects, the construction of the cone as a residence for his sister and the manuscript on Altensam. The narrator can accomplish his task of sorting and ordering Roithamer's papers only if he is able to maintain his independence from his friend, whose ideas and thinking had so overwhelmed him, he says, that he felt "extinguished" ["ausgelöscht"] as an individual (*C* 25-26; *Ko* 38). Like many of Bernhard's protagonists, the narrator associates his newly regained sovereignty with his ability to see clearly: "Now, after such a long time, I think that I am once more in a position to form my own image of the meaning of the objects I look at, instead of Roithamer's image of the scenes at which he and I were looking" (*C* 26; *Ko* 38). By the end of the first chapter, however, the narrator has become increasingly uncertain of the reliability of his own perception. He makes a last effort to assert his sovereignty over the perceived object: "Everything is what it is, that's all....We may see only what we do see which is nothing else but that which we see" (*C* 125-26; *Ko* 172). But this desperate attempt to reaffirm the transparency thesis is contradicted twenty pages later by his own experience. Looking down from his window into Höller's taxidermy workshop, the narrator "sees" Höller: "I actually saw Hoeller sitting there at work with that huge black bird on his lap." But seconds later, Höller appears at the door of his room, "in his nightshirt." The narrator, a prisoner of his own mental projections, had merely imagined him in the workshop: "So he hadn't been in his workshop, in his preservatory, at all, I thought" (*C* 140; *Ko* 192). The scene marks the culmination of a forty-page passage in which the narrator questioned his ability to perform the task he had set for himself while at the same time observing Höller. The two activities are closely related. The collapse of his "objective" vision, demonstrated by his faulty perception of Höller, marks the disintegration of the subject/object dichotomy and thus of his autonomy as knowing subject. Where he had originally stated that part of his task would be to order Roithamer's manuscript and "to reconstitute its original coherence as envisioned by Roithamer" (*C* 10; *Ko* 17), he now claims that any attempt on his part to form Roithamer's papers into "a whole" (*C* 127; *Ko* 175) is out of the question. "Editors," he says, are "criminals" (*C* 128; *Ko* 176). As if to acknowledge his own cognitive impotence, he decides that he will be as cautious and non-intrusive as possible. He will restrict himself to nothing more than "sifting and sorting" (*C* 129; *Ko* 178).

The narrator's experience in the first half of the novel anticipates Roithamer's in the second, which consists of excerpts from his (Roithamer's) papers and is interrupted only two or three times by the narrator. Just as the narrator was unable to assert his cognitive autonomy over the objects of his perception, Roithamer, unable to demonstrate his ability to know the truth either about his sister or about Altensam, must concede that descriptions and facts do not coincide (*C* 265; *Ko* 355). The notion that the manuscript on Altensam "corresponds" to Altensam is just as unfounded as the assertion that the cone "corresponds" to his sister, who is unable to "bear" it and dies shortly after seeing it. The continuity between the two sections of the book is underscored by the fixation on light at the end of both chapters. The word "Lichtung" ["Clearing"], the last word of the novel, recalls the end of the first chapter and the narrator's preoccupation with the lights in his room and in Höller's workshop. Like the end of that chapter, the novel's final scene underscores once again the cognitive impotence of the individual. Roithamer's suicide in the "Lichtung," his final "correction," is an ironic comment on the futile search for objective knowledge and truth, for "light," that dominated his life.[8]

Both sections of the book demonstrate the inscrutability of the world and the impossibility of all but subjective knowledge. Autonomy, the novel suggests, rests not on the preservation of the elusive subject/object dichotomy but on the subject's willingness to abandon the quest for objective knowledge and truth and retreat into his own subjective universe. Although neither the manuscript nor the cone corresponds to reality, they are intimately associated with Roithamer's quest for identity and self-realization. According to the narrator, Roithamer's construction of the cone was his attempt "to realize himself" by means of such an unusual structure (*C* 81; *Ko* 112).[9] And Roithamer himself concedes that the manuscript on Altensam contains only subjective knowledge: "I'm getting closer to Altensam, but I'm not getting closer to Altensam in order to solve its mystery for others; to

---

[8]And is therefore not, in my view, "the final and highest assertion of the autonomy of the self," as David Roberts implies in his "Korrektur der Korrektur? Zu Thomas Bernhards Lebenskunstwerk 'Korrektur,'" *Bernhard: Annäherungen*, ed. Manfred Jurgensen, Queensland Studies in German Language and Literature 8 (Bern: Francke, 1981), p. 208. The end of the novel can also be seen as an ironic comment on Heidegger's notion of "Lichtung" as an opening that "first grants the possibility of truth." See Heidegger, "The End of Philosophy and the Task of Thinking," in *Basic Writings*, ed. David Farrell Krell (New York: Harper and Row, 1977), p. 389.

[9]I believe the cone is therefore more closely associated with the quest for knowledge and the drive for self-realization than it is with Roithamer's incestuous desire for his sister, as other critics have suggested. See for example Bernhard Sorg, *Thomas Bernhard*, Autorenbücher 7 (Munich: Beck, 1977), p. 180; and Alfred Barthofer, "Existenz von der Weltstange. Anmerkungen zu Thomas Bernhards Roman *Korrektur*," *Acta Germanica* 10 (1977): 319-330.

explain it *to myself* is why I am getting closer to Altensam, to *my* Altensam, the one that *I* see" (*C* 242; *Ko* 324-25). Although both undertakings were, in Roithamer's words, "crazed acts," he believes he must nevertheless follow through with them not because they have any objective validity or purpose but because they have become an integral part of himself (cf. *C* 266-67; *Ko* 357).

The futility of the quest for objective knowledge is also the subject of *Auslöschung* (1986).[10] During the first 300 pages of the novel, Murau sits at his desk observing some old photographs of his family. According to the principle that "looking at" leads to "looking through," he believes that by studying these photographic moments, he can grasp the true essence of his parents, brother, and sisters. The photograph of his parents, he asserts, shows them "the way they really were"; the photo is "absolutely authentic" (*A* 27). As far as he is concerned, the photo of his parents *is* his parents just as the mocking faces of his sisters *are* his sisters (*A* 240-41). But Murau also admits that the "truth" and "reality" of the photographs are *his* truth and *his* reality. He doubts, for example, whether his sisters are truly "ridiculous and repulsive," as the photograph of them suggests, but nevertheless decides that he will continue to perceive them this way. Confronted with a choice between objective truth and his own subjective vision, Murau chooses the latter. What matters, he says, is "my truth" (*A* 75): "I was ashamed, but immediately thereafter I had to tell myself that we cannot get out of our own heads, and I insisted that my sisters are *ridiculous and repulsive*" (*A* 106).

Auslöschung suggests not only that knowledge is subjective, but also that all claims to truth are equally valid. When Murau attempts to obtain more information about the accident that killed his parents and brother, he finds that every observer is a prisoner of his own perspective. Although there was only one accident, he soon discovers that there are as many accounts of the event as there are reporters (*A* 414). The notion that these reporters might compare notes and through a process of discussion, argument, and mutual criticism arrive at a consensus is not suggested as a possibility. This perspectivism is reflected in the structure of the novel itself, which presents two contradictory narratives, two opposing versions of the truth, without providing any criteria or method that would enable the reader to decide which, if either, is correct. The first is presented by Murau; the second by Archbishop Spadolini, a close friend of the family and intimate of Murau's mother. Where Murau described Wolfsegg as an "insane hell" (*A* 72-73), Spadolini regards it as a warm and friendly place (*A* 549, 561); Murau's description of his mother as a shallow, calculating, materialistic Philistine is contradicted by Spadolini's portrayal of her as a sensitive, caring, and selfless woman whose death he considers his "greatest loss" (*A* 562). At no time does

---

[10]According to Wendelin Schmidt-Dengler, *Auslöschung* was actually written in 1981-82, which explains some stylistic and thematic similarities with *Correction*. See "Bernhards Attacke auf die ererbte Last der Geschichte," *Kleine Zeitung* (Graz) 27 Feb. 1987: 38. Cited in Ulrich Weinzierl, "Bernhard als Erzieher: Thomas Bernhards *Auslöschung*," *German Quarterly* 63 (1990): 459.

Murau directly confront Spadolini, whom he had praised earlier as a highly credible and reliable individual (*A* 281-82), in order to challenge his perception of Wolfsegg. There is no discussion or give-and-take between them that might help the reader to a determination of the facts. The two accounts are simply presented on a "take-it-or-leave-it" basis. Just as Murau presented *his* truth and *his* reality, Spadolini presents his; as far as the reader is concerned, both versions are equally true (or false). Where *Correction* was still preoccupied with the subject/object dichotomy and by implication with the *possibility* of knowledge, *Auslöschung* suggests that objective knowledge and truth are a matter of indifference. Truth is a function of the protagonist's subjective vision: "true" means "true for me." In Murau's words, we cannot get out of our own heads.

Correction and *Auslöschung* systematically dismantle the traditional tenets of scientific rationality: the separation of subject and object, the notion of truth as correspondence with the facts, the claim that there can be a uniquely rational method of inquiry, and the Popperian idea that critical discussion can contribute to the growth of knowledge.[11] Murau's and Spadolini's contradictory accounts of Wolfsegg are like two radically incommensurable Kuhnian paradigms between which there can be no communication. Where Dürrenmatt, in *Romulus the Great*, attempted to show that individuals with different frameworks can nevertheless communicate and even achieve consensus, Bernhard portrays such frameworks as impenetrable. Like Kuhnian scientists with opposing paradigms, Murau and Spadolini live in different worlds. It is impossible for the reader to decide which account of Wolfsegg is correct because, as Kuhn put it, "there is no neutral algorithm for theory-choice, no systematic decision procedure which, properly applied, must lead each individual...to the same decision." Like the scientist who shifts his allegiance from one paradigm to another "for personal and inarticulate aesthetic considerations," the reader's decision cannot be rationally motivated.[12] In the final analysis, it is arbitrary.[13]

---

[11]Cf. also Karlheinz Rossbacher, who sees in Bernhard's works a rejection of "evolutionary thinking," and Ingrid Petrasch, who maintains that Bernhard's abandonment of the notion of "objective truth" paves the way for a relativistic world view. Rossbacher, "Thomas Bernhard: *Das Kalkwerk* (1970)," *Deutsche Romane des 20. Jahrhunderts: Neue Interpretationen*, ed. Paul Michael Lützeler (Königstein: Athenäum, 1983), p. 376; and Petrasch, *Die Konstitution von Wirklichkeit in der Prosa Thomas Bernhards: Sinnbildlichkeit und groteske Überzeichnung*, Münchener Studien zur literarischen Kultur in Deutschland 2, eds. Renate von Heydebrand, Georg Jäger, Jürgen Scharfschwerdt (Frankfurt: Peter Lang, 1987), pp. 326, 328.

[12]Thomas Kuhn, *The Structure of Scientific Revolutions*, 2nd ed., International Encyclopedia of Unified Science, vol.2, no.2 (Chicago: University of Chicago Press, 1970), pp. 158, 200.

[13]This epistemological uncertainty is, of course, a well-known feature of the modern novel, many of which, according to Wolfgang Iser, deliberately attempt "to provoke the reader into establishing for himself the connections between perception and thought."

The most important consequence of this subjectivism is the demotion of language, which no longer appears as a means of communication, criticism, or analysis but as a "universe-maintenance" device, a tool employed by the protagonist to "justify" and defend his subjective universe against encroachment by objective reality.[14] One of the goals of Murau's manuscript called "Auslöschung" is to uphold his subjective universe by rhetorically "obliterating" all opposing realities: "We all carry a Wolfsegg around with us and have the intention of obliterating it in order to save ourselves, of obliterating it by wanting to write about it, wanting to destroy it" (*A* 199).[15] Two important rhetorical strategies are exaggeration and caricature. According to Reger in *Old Masters: A Comedy* [*Alte Meister: Komödie*], it is only by caricaturing everything around us, by making everything appear ridiculous, including parents and superiors, that we are able to "bear" them (*OM* 57; *AM* 117). Caricature is a powerful survival tactic: "We only control what we ultimately find ridiculous...there is no other, no better, method, he said" (*OM* 59; *AM* 122).

The political rhetoric in Bernhard's novels must also be judged in light of this tactical use of language. In *Auslöschung*, Murau frequently attacks his parents as

---

Narrative uncertainty forces the reader to be skeptical of his or her own cognitive practices, as Hartmut Reinhardt points out in reference to Bernhard: "In the elaboration of the perspective of the narrator and the position of the reader, at issue is first of all the destabilization of a supposed security as the presupposition for a more intense experience." See also Heinrich Lindenmayr, who maintains that the narrative uncertainties in *Das Kalkwerk* are designed to provoke "a reading activity...that is imperative in order to detect Konrad's contradictory argumentation and reasoning." Wolfgang Iser, *The Implied Reader: Patterns of Communication in Prose Fiction from Bunyan to Beckett* (Baltimore: Johns Hopkins University Press, 1974), p. xiv; Reinhardt, "Das kranke Subject," pp. 337-38; 345; and Lindenmayr, *Totalität und Beschränkung: Eine Untersuchung zu Thomas Bernhards Roman "Das Kalkwerk,"* Hochschulschriften: Literaturwissenschaft 50 (Königstein: Forum Academicum in der Verlagsgruppe Athenäum, Hain, Scriptor, Hanstein, 1982), p. 26; See also Jürgen H. Petersen, "Beschreibung einer sinnentleerten Welt. Erzählthematik und Erzählverfahren in Thomas Bernhards Romanen," *Bernhard: Annäherungen*, pp. 143-176; and Gerald Fetz, "Thomas Bernhard and the 'Modern Novel,'" *The Modern German Novel*, ed. Keith Bullivant (Leamington Spa, UK: Berg, 1987), pp. 89-108.

[14]I have adopted the term "universe-maintenance" from Peter L. Berger and Thomas Luckmann, *The Social Construction of Reality: A Treatise in the Sociology of Knowledge* (Garden City, New York: Doubleday, 1966), pp. 104-16.

[15]There is but a small step from rhetorical to physical violence. Murau tells his pupil Gambetti that one must gradually reject everything: "Give up everything, I told Gambetti; reject everything; obliterate everything ultimately, Gambetti" (*A* 212). Where Murau seems content merely to obliterate things by writing about them, however, Gambetti is, in Murau's words, "*the born executor of his fantasies*" (*A* 544). His goal is nothing less, Murau maintains, than "to saw the world to bits and to blow it up" (*A* 543). For an analysis of the rhetorical or "agonistic" function of language in Bernhard see Robert S. Leventhal, "The Rhetoric of Anarcho-Nihilistic Murder: Thomas Bernhard's *Das Kalkwerk*," *Modern Austrian Literature* 21.3-4 (1988): 19-38.

Nazis and condemns Austria as hopelessly National Socialist. At the end of the novel, moreover, he bequeaths Wolfsegg to the Jewish religious community of Vienna. All of this has prompted some critics to see in *Auslöschung* a stinging political critique of Austria.[16] But by describing himself toward the end of the novel as an "artist of exaggeration" (*A* 611), Murau compromises the validity of this critique by suggesting that his political rhetoric was part of his universe-maintenance strategy rather than a form of social discourse. The critical moral thrust of this rhetoric is negated not, as has been suggested, by the fact that Bernhard does not clearly state the principles or values upon which his criticism is based, but by the fact that he does not concede the validity of a *public language* and thus of rational criticism.[17] Discourse exists merely to bolster the individual's subjective universe.

One of the best examples of this use of discourse is *The Loser* [*Der Untergeher*] (1983), whose narrator embarks on a rhetorical tour de force, exploiting the life and death of his friend Wertheimer in an effort to justify his own existence. Unlike Wertheimer, whom their mutual friend Glenn Gould referred to as a "loser" ["Untergeher"] (*L* 16; *U* 26),[18] the narrator portrays himself as a survivor who was able to give up his career as a concert pianist and embark upon a new path. He makes it clear that his account of Wertheimer's life ought not to be regarded as objectively true, maintaining that every judgment is biased and subjective (*L* 132, 149; *U* 190, 213). In other words, Wertheimer is merely an instrument in his attempt to define and justify himself. The narrator feels partially responsible for Wertheimer's death because he did not answer his letters, and he admits that he deserted his friend "in his greatest need" (*L* 55-56; *U* 81). He attempts to exonerate himself from guilt by placing the blame for his death squarely on Wertheimer's own shoulders. Gould's nickname becomes the point of departure for the narrator's attempts to attach labels to his friend that make his suicide appear the inevitable consequence of uncontrollable inner forces. Wertheimer is not only "actually a loser" (*L* 103; *U* 148), he is also "the typical failure" (*L* 107; *U* 154) and finally a hopeless "dead-end type" (*L* 147; *U* 209). For the narrator, Wertheimer's suicide "proves" not only that he was a failure as a musician but also that his "intimate friend" (*L* 99; *U* 142) was incapable of friendship. It was therefore not he, the narrator, who deserted his friend, but Wertheimer who deserted the narrator:

[16]Rolf Michaelis describes the novel as "a political lampoon" and Ulrich Weinzierl sees it as Bernhard's "only emphatically political book." See Michaelis, "Vernichtungsjubel. Thomas Bernhards monumentales Prosawerk *Auslöschung* — *Ein Zerfall*. Politisches Pamphlet und Roman der Trauer," *Die Zeit* 3 Oct. 1986, Beilage: 3, and Weinzierl, p. 459.

[17]Cf. Norbert Leser, "Warum Bernhard (noch) kein Moralist ist," *profil* (Vienna) 43 (21 Oct. 1985): 74.

[18]The term "Untergeher," a neologism, defies literal translation into English but has the sense of "one fated to fail or perish."

> In theory he was our friend, that is my friend and Glenn's, in practice he never
> was, I thought, for he lacked everything necessary for *actual* friendship, as he did
> for musical virtuosity, as his suicide indicates, I thought. The so-called bottom line
> is *he* killed himself, not *I*, I thought... (*L* 114; *U* 164).

The narrator uses his friend's suicide as a foil for his own search for identity and
self-realization. Wertheimer's "failure" is evidence for his "success." The fact that
he is alive and Wertheimer is dead "proves" that he made the right choice in
abandoning his career as a pianist. The use of "scientific" or analytical language
(more evident in the German: "wie sein Selbstmord beweist"; "Fazit ist...") con-
fers an air of objectivity and inevitability on his conclusions.[19] If Wertheimer is
a loser, he is a "philosopher" (*L* 17; *U* 26) and a "philosophical worldview artist"
(*L* 50; *U* 74). The narrator constructs his subjective universe over Wertheimer's
grave. It is no wonder that he describes his planned visit to Wertheimer's hunting
lodge as "grave robbery" (*L* 35; *U* 53).

Despite their attempts to establish themselves in their subjective universes, few
of Bernhard's protagonists are able to maintain their subjective vision for very
long. Although they are reluctant to acknowledge it, few can escape the fact that
there is another reality and another truth beyond that which they have created for
themselves. By admitting that their descriptions and judgments were wrong,
Roithamer and the narrator of *The Loser* both implied the existence of "right"
descriptions and judgments.[20] Similarly, Murau's description of himself as an
"artist of exaggeration" implies the existence of an objective standard against
which exaggerations can be judged as such. Roithamer's assertion that one should
be prepared to abandon every "unsuitable" society in order to find comfort and
"clarity" within oneself is not a recommendation that most of Bernhard's
protagonists can easily put into practice (*C* 264; *Ko* 354); their attempts to define
themselves in terms of their subjective universes are accompanied by isolation and
an oppressive *Alleinsein*. Perhaps as a result, the social dimension plays a more
prominent role in the later novels.

In *Concrete* [*Beton*] (1982), Rudolf's conspicuous failure as an observer and
his ineptitude as a creator of his own universe render him a caricature of earlier
figures such as Roithamer or Murau. In contrast to the extraordinary perceptive
skills alleged by these characters, Rudolf cannot see beyond the confines of his
own house:

---

[19]That such language is purely tactical is demonstrated, for example, by the absurdity of
Reger's claim in *Old Masters* that it is "scientifically established" that the Viennese use soap
and change their underwear only once a week (*OM* 83; *AM* 167).

[20]The narrator of *The Loser* maintains that we "portray and judge people only in false
terms" (*L* 149; *U* 213), and Roithamer realizes "that I'd described everything all wrong
[falsch], for the opposite is true...[denn es ist das Entgegengesetzte...]" (*C* 266; *Ko* 356).

> I leant against the sill and tried, by continuous concentration, to descry the wall
> on the other side of the yard, but despite the most intense concentration I couldn't
> make it out. Only twenty yards away and I can't see the wall! (*Co* 35; *B* 51).

Where earlier works stressed the relationship between observer and observed,
Rudolf, wherever he looks, sees only himself. Standing in his room, Rudolf
observes "Rudolf" sitting at his writing desk (*Co* 14, 103; *B* 22, 142). Nor is his
attempt to define himself by retreating into a subjective universe successful: he is
unable to complete his life's work, a study of Felix Mendelssohn, and he remains
dependent on his worldly sister Elisabeth, of whom he says, "It would be
impossible to imagine a person more hostile to anything intellectual than my sister"
(*Co* 6-7; *B* 12), but on whom he depends to rescue him "from the hell of being
alone" (*Co* 27; *B* 39).

The social dimension in the novel is represented by Elisabeth and Anna Härdtl,
a young woman whom Rudolf met a year and a half earlier in Palma. A successful
business woman, gifted conversationalist, and skillful politician who quickly
masters every social situation, Elisabeth is, in Rudolf's words, "the realistic
person" while he is "the imaginative one" ["der phantastische"] (*Co* 36; *B* 52).
Elisabeth is Rudolf's link to the outside world.[21] She attempts to coax her "little
brother" out of his "morgue" ["Gruft"] (*Co* 18; *B* 27) and into life. Anna Härdtl's
suicide, by contrast, reminds him of the reality of death, an awareness that has
been suppressed by his effete existence and neurotic preoccupations with his own
illness. The two women thus represent the two forces that unite all men and
women: the bond to each other and the knowledge of their own mortality. The
importance of the two women for Rudolf's life is evident in the fact that he cannot
escape either of them: he needs his sister just as he inexplicably "needed" to return
to the cemetery in Palma to discover the name "Anna Härdtl" on the tomb.
Elisabeth, who deals in real estate, and Anna Härdtl, who ends in a concrete vault,
both remind him of the "hard" facts of objective reality. They point to the reality
of human existence in which life is not a "morgue" and death is not merely a
word.

In *Woodcutters* [*Holzfällen*] (1984), the notion that the observer occupies a
privileged position vis-a-vis the object or that he can mold the object according to
his subjective vision is contradicted by the fact that the subject, the narrator, is
inextricably bound to the object, the society whose duplicity and empty conventions he so ruthlessly criticizes throughout the novel. Although he attempts to
establish his sovereignty over the other dinner guests by ruthlessly "looking
through" them, the narrator's ability to know them fails on two occasions: he
misjudges John, who is not the dissolute human being he had thought but "a good
man" (*W* 40, 65; *H* 70, 114), as well as the actor from the Burgtheater, whom he
considered a "mindless ham" (*W* 15; *H* 28) but who transforms himself before his

---

[21]Peter Buchka describes Elisabeth as "the embodiment of the reality principle."
"Nörgelei als Widerstand. Thomas Bernhards neues Prosabuch *Beton*," *Süddeutsche Zeitung*
6 Oct. 1982.

eyes "from a gargoyle into a philosophical human being, from a repellent stage character into a real person" (*W* 172-73; *H* 306). Nor is he able to secure his autonomy by ensconcing himself in his own subjective universe. He cannot avoid participating in social rituals and thereby acknowledging that he is a member of the very society he professes to despise. Before leaving the Gentzgasse, he kisses the detested Frau Auersberger on the forehead as he did twenty years before and tells her the miserable evening had been a pleasure, only to chide himself immediately thereafter for being as hypocritical as everyone else (*W* 177-78; *H* 315). Like the actor, the narrator is at once *Figur* and *Mensch*, a performer of socially prescribed roles as well as an individual.[22] He is forced to accept the fact that he is member of a community and "that these are my people and will always be my people" (*W* 181; *H* 321). Rather than occupying a privileged position vis-a-vis the world, the novel suggests that the observer is an intrinsic part of it.

In *Old Masters* [*Alte Meister*] (1985), Reger applies this insight to painting. He sees the "old masters" in Vienna's Kunsthistorisches Museum not as privileged observers with special access to the "truth" but as individuals struggling to come to terms with their world. Every work by the old masters is deficient and full of "errors"; every one of them is a "failure" who never succeeded in painting "a one-hundred-percent picture of genius" (*OM* 152; *AM* 302-03). The paintings contain "only lies and mendacity without reality and truth" (*OM* 28; *AM* 61). Each one, he maintains, is little more than a "paltry attempt at survival" and as such an expression of man's "absolute helplessness" (*OM* 151; *AM* 301, 303). The paintings of the old masters are not perfect, detached *objets d'art* but works that bear witness to their creators' involvement in life. The attempt to judge the paintings by absolute standards deprives them of this human dimension. Art is not intended "for total viewing or for total listening or for total reading" (*OM* 33; *AM* 70), Reger maintains. This totalizing vision destroys "the most beautiful and the most useful things in the world" (*OM* 32; *AM* 68). Art is not valuable because it is "true" or because it portrays the "essence" of the world, but because of its beauty and usefulness, its human qualities. In contrast to Bernhard's earlier protagonists, such as Roithamer, who claimed to have perceived the essence of his sister, or Murau, who claimed to "see" the "truth and reality" of his parents, sisters, and brother, Reger suggests that the drive to know the "essence" of a thing, this "mechanism of dissection and disintegration" (*OM* 113; *AM* 226), is misguided and inhumane. Just as the paintings are full of errors and faults but nevertheless are still worth experiencing, so too is life. After his wife's death, Reger returns to the society that offers him the only possibility of survival: "We hate people and yet we want to be with them because only with people and among

---

[22]Cf. Gerhard Pail, who comments on "the possibility of differentiating two different selves in the narrator: the specifically observing and evaluating self and a self oriented toward social norms and conventions." "Perspektivität in Thomas Bernhards *Holzfällen*," *Modern Austrian Literature* 21.3-4 (1988): 56.

people do we stand a chance of carrying on without going insane" (*OM* 145-46; *AM* 291).

These novels suggest communicative interaction as an alternative to the monologic search for truth and for self-realization that characterized most of Bernhard's earlier novels, but once again his protagonists are unable to escape from their subjective universes. Communication remains impossible. The desire for human interaction, if it is articulated at all, is expressed only obliquely, as something that is simultaneously desired and spurned. In this respect, the situation of Bernhard's protagonists is similar to that of the protagonist of a novel written a century earlier: Des Esseintes in Huysmans's *Against the Grain* (1884). In this first novel of European decadence, Des Esseintes attempted to withdraw from the world and lead a completely self-sufficient aesthetic existence. Commenting on the book, one reviewer remarked that the only choice left to the author of such a work was that between the muzzle of a pistol or the foot of the cross.[23] Bernhard's protagonists are confronted with a similar choice, except that the foot of the cross is replaced by a reluctant acknowledgment that they are, whether they like it or not, members of a communicatively supported collective.

[23]Cited by J. K. Huysmans, "Preface Written Twenty Years After the Novel," *Against the Grain* (*A Rebours*) (1931; New York: Dover, 1969), p. xlix.

4 Science, Rationality, and the Disintegration of the Public Sphere: Gerhard Roth

DESPITE ITS TITLE, Gerhard Roth's (b. 1942) early experimental novel *die autobiographie des albert einstein* (1972) has little to do with the life of the physicist born in Ulm in 1879. Einstein's influence can be found instead in a number references to the relationship between the mind and the world that, despite their apparent radicality, are in fact entirely consistent with Einstein's (and Popper's) views on the subject. Roth's einstein speaks of the arbitrariness of causality, claims that there are no necessary connections between things, and asserts that language disguises reality. Science, he maintains, creates its own truth; it produces "a home-made truth." The reality of the natural sciences, he logically and correctly concludes, is not real.[1] Like Einstein and Popper, Roth's protagonist regards scientific theories as artificial constructs and scientific "truth" as a human invention, but he differs with them in the value he places on such theorizing. Where Einstein and most scientists would regard such constructs as conjectures in an ongoing process of trial and error, Roth's protagonist sees them as part of a web of imposed metanarratives that determine our thinking. Rather than bring us closer to the truth, scientific rationality merely obfuscates it.

Scientific rationality is part of a reigning ideology that Roth believes has transformed the lifeworld into an impenetrable system of entrenched errors, obliterating all authentic meanings. "We live in a world of shams, errors, and false facts....The world is topsy-turvy, and the only closed, impenetrable system in power is the system of shams," he stated in a recent article.[2] Language and thought, he wrote in another essay, have been "colonized" by the media with the result that human beings have become "thinking illiterates."[3] "If we want to

[1]Gerhard Roth, *die autobiographie des albert einstein: Fünf Kurzromane* (Frankfurt: Fischer, 1972), pp. 41, 75. All translations throughout are my own.

[2]Roth, "Labyrinth der Fälschungen" [Labyrinth of Shams], *Die Zeit* 21 Jan. 1988: 50.

[3]Roth, "Das allmähliche Verstummen der Sprache" [Language Gradually Grows Silent], *Die Zeit* 16 Oct. 1987: 68.

encounter ourselves, we discover an eternal Don Quichotte who is duped as much by the windmills in his own head as by the fata morgana of the outside world." Roth describes a world in which meaningful communicative interaction has become impossible. It is a world in which the public sphere, as the locus of discourse free of domination, has disintegrated. In this world, everything is simply a matter of form: "The uniform of the famous Sergeant Köpenick shows how much what is 'right' depends on arrangements. Wrong becomes right without resistance, if can only be made to fit seamlessly."[4]

Roth's work is a confrontation with this world of "shams, errors, and false facts." It is also a search for a new domination-free language that would make possible the articulation of more authentic meanings, which Roth believes exist beyond the shams and deceptions.[5] The quest for this language leads him to the private sphere. But the language of this sphere is an intensely personal and idiosyncratic one. Roth's protagonists are thus caught between a world of falsifications, where real communication is impossible, and a private world, where they are also linguistically isolated. His quest for a purified language that would transform false facts into truths and make errors right leads him from the social world to a private realm of dreams, mysticism, or even madness.

In this chapter, I shall discuss four works that are part of the as yet incomplete cycle that Roth has titled "Die Archive des Schweigens" [The Archives of Silence]. These are: *Der stille Ozean* [The Silent Ocean] (1980), *Landläufiger Tod* [Common Death] (1984), *Am Abgrund* [At the Abyss] (1986), and *Der Untersuchungsrichter: Die Geschichte eines Entwurfs* [The Examining Judge: The History of a Sketch] (1988).[6] The works are connected primarily by character. Dr. Ascher, the central figure of *Der stille Ozean*, reappears in *Landläufiger Tod*, where two new characters, Franz Lindner and his friend Alois Jenner, are also introduced. Jenner, a pathological murderer, becomes the central figure in *Am Abgrund* (1986), which also introduces a new character, the examining judge Sonnenberg. Sonnenberg then becomes the central figure of the next book of the cycle, *Der Untersuchungsrichter*.

In *Der stille Ozean*, Dr. Ascher's move from Vienna to the Styrian countryside to escape the repercussions of a malpractice suit precipitates a search for those two things that Roth claims are most important to him as a writer: "survival and

---

[4]Last two quotations are taken from "Labyrinth der Fälschungen," p. 50.

[5]There is, he maintains, a "cosmic principle" in nature that can be glimpsed, for example, in the organized world of bees. See Roth, *Über Bienen. Mit Fotos von Franz Killmeyer* [On Bees. With Photographs by Franz Killmeyer] (Vienna: Jugend und Volk, 1989), p. 5.

[6]Also included in the cycle are *Im tiefen Österreich* [In the Depths of Austria] (1990), a collection of photographs, *Eine Reise in das Innere von Wien* [A Journey to the Center of Vienna] (1991), a collection of essays, and, most recently published, a book entitled *Die Geschichte der Dunkelheit* [The History of Darkness] (1991).

meaning" ["Überleben und Sinn"].[7] These two goals are related, for survival depends on the individual's ability to articulate a meaning for his or her life. In Roth's works, finding this meaning often entails establishing contact with another, deeper reality that is frequently associated with death.[8] In *Der stille Ozean*, this is made clear during one of several hunting scenes in the novel. When a hound catches a hare, it appears to Dr. Ascher as if the dog had fetched it "from another reality" and as if its removal from that reality were the cause of its death.[9] The hare thus comes to symbolize the connection between these two worlds. Later, Dr. Ascher accepts death as "the strangest and most distant thing" he knows, but also as "the most self-evident thing" (181). In doing so, he is able to integrate death and thus an awareness of this other reality into his life. Although his motivations are not entirely clear, this insight seems to be closely connected with his decision to remain in the village and dedicate his life to caring for its inhabitants. In deciding to stay in the village, he shows that the everyday world can be united with a deeper reality and sense of purpose. Significantly, he is able to do this by accepting a social role, that of doctor. His decision implies that "meaning and survival" can be found in community with others through an acknowledgment of one's participation in a web of communicative action.[10]

Der stille Ozean is thus far the only work in the "Archives of Silence" in which a commitment to society is suggested as a response to the protagonist's search for meaning. In the next novel, his magnum opus, *Landläufiger Tod* (1984), Roth rejects this solution. As if to make this retraction absolutely clear, he has Dr. Ascher appear in *Landläufiger Tod* once more, and in a section of the novel that gives the work its title, Ascher kills himself in a state of weary despair. As the title implies, death has become "common," and the chasm in Roth's work between the everyday reality of falsifications and the increasingly distant world of meanings and possibilities becomes deeper and wider than ever.

[7]"Keine Sehnsucht nach Stillstand. Mit Gerhard Roth sprach Kurt Wimmer," *Kleine Zeitung* (Graz) 5 June 1977.

[8]This was also true of the present novel's three predecessors, *Der große Horizont* [The Vast Horizon] (1974), *Ein neuer Morgen* [A New Morning] (1976), and *Winterreise* [Winter Journey] (1978), where the other reality often appeared as a rupture in the fabric of daily life or as an other-worldly vision.

[9]*Der stille Ozean* (Frankfurt: Fischer, 1980), p. 47.

[10]Some critics have found this decision to be psychologically unmotivated, claiming that it appears "tacked on" to the novel. See for example Sylvia Adrian, "Ich will ein Erzähler sein," *Frankfurter Hefte* Feb. 1981: 67-68, or Günter Blöcker, "Ein kündiger Protokollant seelischer Irritationen. Gerhard Roths Roman *Der stille Ozean*," *Frankfurter Allgemeine* 22 March 1980. Sigrid Bauschinger, by contrast, sees Ascher's decision as a deliberate return "to the world and to his work." "Gerhard Roth," in *Major Figures of Contemporary Austrian Literature*, ed. Donald G. Daviau (New York, Berne: Peter Lang, 1987), p. 354. My point is that, whatever his motivations might be, Ascher realizes an important life decision by returning to society.

Landläufiger Tod, a sprawling work of nearly 800 pages, is divided into seven books, which are "narrated" by Franz Lindner, a mute beekeeper. The first book, "Dunkle Erinnerung" [Dark Recollection], begins with "Circus Saluti," a story that Roth originally published separately in 1981, and ends with the story of Dr. Ascher's suicide. Dr. Ascher's death seems to have deeply affected Lindner, for the second book, "Berichte aus dem Labyrinth" [Reports from the Labyrinth], finds him in an asylum. With almost 400 pages, the third book, "Mikrokosmos," is clearly the novel's centerpiece. The "microcosm" is the world of the Styrian village in which Lindner lives.[11] Taken from Lindner's "papers," the book records events and experiences by Lindner and other villagers from the First World War to the present. The fourth book, "Aufbruch ins Unbekannte" [Departure for the Unknown], relates the fantastic events surrounding the death of the local military general and a mystical experience of the undertaker's assistant. The fifth book consists of fairy tales recorded by Lindner and the sixth contains excerpts from Lindner's diary. The final book contains sketches by Günter Brus.

The circus that opens the novel is a metaphor for the social world, where falsifications, deceptions, and illusions are taken for reality and truth. As the circus model makes clear, these illusions are not innocuous; they are imposed by those with power and authority, and they are inescapable. In the circus, the most obvious victims of this power are the performing animals. Their behavior is not their own but that of their trainers, who, as Lindner's friend Jenner says, "speak" through them.[12] The parallel between the animals, who are unaware of their "humiliation" (34), and human beings, who are unaware of the illusions thrust upon them, becomes apparent when the circus director forces a hypnotized young man to cut off the head of a chicken, place it in his mouth, and flutter about like a hen. Within the circus, the director has complete power to determine what is real or unreal. "Whereas I usually create the impression that the unreal is real, in this trick I have transformed reality into unreality," he says of the chicken stunt (50). He insists that people want to be "led around by the nose" and that the circus makes them receptive for illusions (24). Franz Lindner counters that the circus merely exploits the fact that people have the capacity to dream and indeed to live in their dreams. But the director refuses to grant even the freedom of dreams, maintaining that they, too, have been predetermined: "I present a dream to them and they dream along. All the dreams dreamt by these people have been dreamt and lived long before" (25).

---

[11]Roth spent several years living in a village in western Styria, and many of the personalities and incidents described in the novel are based on fact. See Roth's bilingual publication *On the Boarderline* [sic]: *A Documentary Record. Grenzland: Ein dokumentarisches Protokoll* (Vienna: Hannibal, 1981). See also Walter Grond, "Gerhard Roths *Landläufiger Tod*. Zur Genese eines Romans," *manuskripte: Zeitschrift für Literatur* 29.105 (1989): 83-91.

[12]*Landläufiger Tod* (Frankfurt: Fischer, 1984), p. 29. Further references to the novel will be given in the text.

The circus director symbolizes the power of the dominant ideology to control every aspect of life, including the private sphere. Another representative of this power is Lindner's doctor, who attempts to make Lindner's dreams conform to the "laws" of the waking world. Attempts to explain dreams, Lindner believes, are merely attempts to impose an external "grammar" on a language that has its own rules. After translating the dream in accordance with this grammar, the doctor may believe he has understood it, but in fact he has simply imposed an arbitrary system upon it that has no claim to objectivity or truth. Like the trainers who "speak" through the circus animals, the doctor, says Lindner, simply makes the dream "perform" according to his own rules: "Of course, one can make dreams serve certain purposes, in the same way one trains an elephant or a monkey" (509). The whole process is self-referential, the doctor believing he has made progress when he has found his own preconceived ideas confirmed. Based on the "proofs" he has thus gleaned from his research, the doctor decides what is normal and what is abnormal, just as the circus director determined what was real and what was illusion. But like the circus, this whole process is based on deception and sleight-of-hand. The doctor gains no real insights into his patient or his dreams. As Lindner puts it, he sees the world with the eyes of a clockmaker observing a whale (509). Moreover, in deciding what is normal or abnormal, the doctor is an unwitting agent of authority. As far as his thinking is concerned, Lindner tells him, he is like a swimmer pulled along by the "ruling current" (570). The doctor is part of the duplicitous system that characterizes society. What he regards as "proofs" are actually "false facts"; his "knowledge" is merely prejudice.[13]

Although the doctor presents his method as neutral and objective, it is in fact a form of hegemony and domination. References to "laws" and "proofs" are merely attempts to lend legitimacy to arbitrary procedures by making them appear "scientific." But as the narrator of *Der Untersuchungsrichter* (1988) makes clear, science is neither objective nor neutral; it is invested with interests. The logic of science, he declares, is the logic of destruction: "We think, so to speak, in dead objects, in dyed microscopic slide preparations...we dissect. Our methods of thinking are *incisions*."[14] In *Am Abgrund* (1986), this destructive rationality is exemplified in the murderer Alois Jenner and in the image of the slaughterhouse. In its execution, Jenner's crime — he coldly murdered an elderly couple in a moment of unmotivated brutality — parallels the means-to-ends efficiency of the slaughterhouse he visits shortly thereafter. The butcher, who quickly dispatches the animals with a shot to the head, recalls the cold indifference with which Jenner murdered

---

[13]This discussion is based on an analysis of two sections of the novel: "Traumlogik" [Dream Logic] (507-12) and "Die Krankheit im Geiste" [The Sickness in the Mind] (569-73). The notion of examinations as tools of normalization shows the strong influence of Michel Foucault on Roth's thinking. See Foucault, *Discipline and Punish: The Birth of the Prison* (New York: Pantheon, 1977). See also note 17 below.

[14]Roth, *Der Untersuchungsrichter: Die Geschichte eines Entwurfs* (Frankfurt: Fischer, 1988), p. 133. Further references will be indicated in the text.

his victims in the same way. Both killers remain emotionally aloof and "completely calm."[15] The butcher informs Jenner that the efficient killing and dismemberment of the animals is the result of decades, if not centuries, of development. Every detail of the operation is planned; nothing is left to chance (68). The efficient slaughtering technology is the transformation of the uncompromising logic of science into practical terms. In their calculated efficiency, both killers represent concrete examples of what the narrator of *Der Untersuchungsrichter* refers to as "'correct thinking,'" that dominant mode of thought that, he continues, has transformed the world into the "slaughterhouse" it has become (172).

This "correct thinking" includes mathematics, upon which modern science is based, as well as a number of other ideas that are often associated with scientific rationality, for example, the notion that by proceeding logically and methodically goals will be reached; that the accumulation of evidence will lead to certain conclusions about reality; or that proofs imply truth. These principles are embodied in the structure of criminal trials, which play a prominent role in *Am Abgrund* and *Der Untersuchungsrichter*. In a trial, the prosecutor presents a theory, supported by evidence, about a crime. This theory is then subjected to criticism by the defense, which may present counter-evidence. In this process of theory-building and mutual criticism, the circumstances surrounding the crime become clear. Ideally, the trial thus becomes "a metaphor for the road to truth as well as for that to justice."[16] In these two works, however, trials are not roads to the truth but meaningless formalities. For the murderer Alois Jenner, who admires geometric figures for their "purity" (*Am Abgrund* 144), a trial is a kind of mathematical problem solving. "It was in no way a question of doing justice to a human being, a perpetrator, a victim, an innocent person but of accommodating public opinion and the justice system" (140), he says as he calmly watches a man being convicted for a crime that he, Jenner, committed. Echoing Jenner's view, the narrator of *Der Untersuchungsrichter* maintains that trials are a "ritual," more concerned with the right language than with determining the facts (11). Similarly, the examining judge Sonnenberg, like Jenner, rejects the notion that a court procedure can discern the truth. There are, he maintains, no compelling conclusions; one can almost always prove the opposite. Proofs are for "stupid people" (*Der Untersuchungsrichter* 26). What he constructs from his interrogations and examinations, he says, is simply "the model of coherency," a "geometric figure" that is then presented as "reality" (42).

The criticism of rationality and science in these books recalls similar analyses by Habermas, Kuhn, Feyerabend, and Aronowitz as well as earlier critiques by

---

[15]Roth, *Am Abgrund* (Frankfurt: Fischer, 1986), pp. 36, 66. Further references will be given in the text.

[16]Ralf Dahrendorf, *Society and Democracy in Germany* (1967; New York: Norton, 1979), p. 146.

members of the Frankfurt School.[17] Roth's fictional analyses suggest that the rules of logic and rationality are not necessary but contingent; that methods of inquiry are self-referential; that knowledge is a form of power; that science is governed by a cognitive interest in domination and control; and that reality is an (arbitrary) construct. Thinking "correctly" in accordance with established principles of logic and science can therefore offer no guarantee of progress toward the truth. This is the lesson contained in two favorite stories related by the examining judge in *Am Abgrund*. The first story describes the discovery of the source of the Nile, the second the adventures of an explorer who, while making his way through the African jungle, stumbles by chance upon a German colleague long given up for dead. Where the first discovery was based on planning ("'The goal of our journey was reached,' the report had ended"), the second discovery results from "an unbelievable coincidence" (*Am Abgrund* 115-16). The lesson is clear: a rationally (that is, "correctly") planned scientific expedition is no more likely to lead to a momentous discovery than blind chance.

According to the narrator of *Der Untersuchungsrichter*, there can be no truly "correct thinking" because the mind itself is biased. Thinking, he says, is like a bird trapped in a room that repeatedly tries to fly through a glass window until it kills itself (73). Taking Lindner's criticism of his doctor's self-confirming procedures one step further, he maintains that thought itself is self-referential. What the mind regards as knowledge is in fact predetermined by the structure of the brain: "The brain is a dim-witted, cunning cardshark. In the end, it believes in its own capabilities as if it had not been playing with marked cards" (55). There is no Archimedean point outside the mind that could provide a guarantee for cognitive processes. There can thus be no truly "objective" knowledge.

This idea is reflected formally in the insecurity of the narrator of *Der Untersuchungsrichter*. Although he presents himself as the author of the book, he cannot maintain his position as narrator and tell his story. He regularly interrupts the narrative in order to talk about himself, to discuss his authorial intentions ("This is not a report about an illness; it is not a description of symptoms. It is not my intention to expose a confused state" [73]), or to theorize about problems

---

[17]Habermas, Kuhn, Feyerabend, and Aronowitz were discussed in the introduction. On the Frankfurt School and its critique of the instrumentality of scientific rationality see esp. Max Horkheimer and Theodor Adorno, *Dialectic of Enlightenment*, trans. John Cumming (1944; New York: Continuum, 1987). See also Herbert Marcuse, *One-Dimensional Man: Studies in the Ideology of Advanced Industrial Society*. (Boston: Beacon Press, 1964), esp. chapter 6: "From Negative to Positive Thinking: Technological Rationality and the Logic of Domination," and Marcuse, "On Science and Phenomenology," in *The Essential Frankfurt School Reader*, eds. Andrew Arato and Eike Gebhardt (New York: Continuum, 1982), pp. 466-76. The association of knowledge with power also shows once again the strong influence of Michel Foucault. On Foucault's influence in *Der Untersuchungsrichter* see Klaus-Peter Philippi, "Das Leben ist der kurze Moment des Sturzes. Neue Wahrnehmungsprosa von Gerhard Roth: Ein Untersuchungsrichter zwischen Lüge und Gewalt," *Rheinischer Merkur/Christ und Welt* 25 March 1988, and Georg Pichler, "Der Gimpel pfeift im Pfirsichgeblüh. Gerhard Roths *Untersuchungsrichter*," *Die Presse* (Vienna) 4/5 June 1988, Beilage: 8.

presented in the novel. Rather than demonstrate his omniscience, however, this activity disguises his cognitive uncertainty. He is unable to maintain his epistemic sovereignty over the object of his investigation and fulfill his narrative obligations, namely, to organize the material before him into a coherent whole. As a result, the story does not "end"; he simply stops telling it. The book never becomes a novel; it remains an unfinished "sketch."

The narrator's failure to assert his epistemic authority and complete the novel is a formal demonstration of the principle that there are no overarching, objective criteria that can be used to privilege one interpretation of reality over another. "Reality" is determined by each individual's conceptual framework. In *Landläufiger Tod*, the doctor will never understand the different world that Lindner inhabits because his perception is determined by the norms of society. He will always observe his patient like the hapless clockmaker trying to understand the whale. In a section of the novel entitled "Die Sehweise der Biene" [The Vision of Bees], Lindner finds evidence for this incompatibility in nature itself. Because they perceive colors differently from human beings, bees exist in a different world: "That means that creatures that perceive different waves of the spectrum than we do live in a different world with other manifestations and possibly other beings" (220). The world does not merely *appear* different to the bees; it *is* different. Similarly, the world inhabited by Lindner *is* different from that of his doctor. They will never agree what "reality" is. Their opposing theories are, in Kuhn's terms, radically incommensurable: there is no common conceptual ground between them that would allow for the possibility of mutual understanding, or even of meaningful communication.

The tension between a socially sanctioned and a private reality is reflected in the third book of *Landläufiger Tod* in schizophrenic behavior on the part of several characters, suggesting that each of them lives in two worlds at once, in the official one and in an incomprehensible private reality with its own standards and norms. Hence, the minds and actions of these figures seem to inhabit different realms. There is the "automatic man" who marches like a robot through the countryside oblivious to his surroundings; or the man who is uncertain whether he is leading his own life or that of his twin brother; or the Russian prisoner of war who can flawlessly repeat any German sentences he hears without understanding a word he is saying; or the murderer who "watches" himself strangle an old man as if he were someone else and then later insists that the incident had nothing to do with him.[18] Where there is no shared notion of reality, these incidents suggest, there can be no shared meanings and no common conception of what it means to be a human being.

There can also be no shared notion of truth and no universal standards of moral behavior. This is made clear in one of the longest and most compelling sections of

---

[18]See the following sections of the novel: "Totenstill" [Deathly Still] (57-77); "Lebenslauf eines Zwillingspaares" [The Life of a Pair of Twins] (422-24); "Der Russe" [The Russian] (347-54); and "Der Blick eines Mörders" [The Gaze of a Murderer] (306-08).

book three, a story from the Second World War entitled "Hahnlosers Ende." Hahnloser, a partisan, forces the village priest to shoot a soldier on leave in the village, thus making it appear as if the priest were one of the partisans and making it impossible for him to implicate Hahnloser without also accusing himself. Although the priest is confident that the police would believe his statements over those of Hahnloser, cowardice, pride, and an unwillingness to be responsible for another death, namely Hahnloser's, convince him to lie when asked by the police whether he recognized anyone. "Whom would the truth benefit?" (381), he asks himself. This lie marks a turning point in the priest's life. The truth — that he shot the young soldier — is the product of Hahnloser's treachery. Truth and deception have become so enmeshed that it seems pointless to speak of The Truth. Truth is contingent upon one's perspective; the value of "telling the truth" is relative to the situation at hand. As a result, the priest loses the moral ability to locate himself unambiguously in the world. He can no longer function as an autonomous moral agent, a fact that is reflected, as in the other figures described above, in schizophrenic thinking: "His understanding extended only to a certain point. Although he did not deny everything that had happened, he could nevertheless assert with complete conviction that he had not been a part of these events" (381). The world for the priest has become "absurd" (383); the lie has transformed him, as he says, into "lifeless material" (379). Like the automatic man, he has become a thing.

This view of human beings contrasts sharply with the one presented at the end of *Der stille Ozean*, where Dr. Ascher was able to find a purpose for his life by accepting his role as a contributing member of a community. In *Landläufiger Tod*, human beings have no connection to a communicatively supported collective. Each is enclosed within his own conceptual system, and, if Lindner's example of the bees is accepted, within his own hermetic world. There can be no agreement on what constitutes objective reality because there is no common language with which to refer to it. There are no shared, authentic meanings because public meanings are obscure or are regarded as alien. And there is no meaningful human contact because there are no autonomous subjects. The world in *Landläufiger Tod* is a place without communicative interaction. In contrast to the path taken by Dr. Ascher in *Der stille Ozean*, a deeper meaning can be found not in a turn to one's fellow man but, the novel suggests, by withdrawing, like Franz Lindner, into a world of dreams or madness.[19]

In contrast to the falsifications and deceptions of the social world, this inner world, Roth suggests, offers the possibility of an unobstructed vision. Such a vision is presented in a section of *Landläufiger Tod* entitled "Zwischen Himmel und Erde" [Between Heaven and Earth], in which an intuitive understanding of the deep truths of the universe descends upon the undertaker's assistant. During this mystical experience, the divisions and categories that rational thought normally imposes on the world are dissolved. Mind and body, self and other, past, present,

---

[19]At one point Lindner asserts that withdrawal into one's own head offers the only escape from thoughts of suicide. See p. 330.

and future appear to him in a unified vision of the world. The earth is a mind and he is one of its thoughts; the worlds he experiences are not only outside him, but also within him. He hears the "mighty music of the universe" (600) and gains an intuitive understanding of the laws of nature: "Without seeing the earth, he could now understand the laws according to which it was constructed" (602). The undertaker experiences the utopian coincidence of perception and knowledge. The mind is a mirror in which the truths of the universe are reflected without the distortions imposed upon human inquiry by society, history, or the mind itself. The world, for once, is transparent.

The desire for such transparency is also responsible for Roth's fascination with madness. "I regard the so-called mentally ill as the only people with dignity," he wrote in 1980.[20] The language of madness, he maintains, can be the source of a more authentic perspective. In a review of the poetry of Ernst Herbeck, who has spent most of his life in an asylum, Roth writes:

> This poet speaks to us not from a world of madness, but from one of isolation; not from a world of 'normalcy' (by which are tacitly meant all the lies that are necessary to uphold the existing order); he speaks to us from a world of sharpened but wounded senses.

Herbeck, he continues, has "microscopic eyes" that can see "into the interior of things."[21] In another article, Roth praises the thinking of the (so-called) mentally ill as "wonder-ful" ["wunder-voll"] and contrasts the immediacy of their language with that of the media, which has lost its "dignity and independence."[22] In *Landläufiger Tod*, such a language can also be found in those fantastic passages — "Die Schöpfung," "Das gefrorene Paradies," "Das Alter der Zeit" [The Creation, The Frozen Paradise, The Age of Time] — written by the allegedly mad Franz Lindner. In these sections, language is decentered or dislocated; it is "freed" of the customary restraints of coherency and logic in order to make possible a new vision of the world.[23]

---

[20]"Selbstgespräch (I)" [Conversation with Myself (I)] in Roth, *Die schönen Bilder beim Trabrennen* [Lovely Pictures at the Trotters] (Frankfurt: Fischer, 1982), p. 10. This sentiment is also echoed by the narrator of *Der Untersuchungsrichter*, who maintains that we should defend "the dignity of the idiot." Earlier in the novel, the narrator said it was frequently his secret wish to be locked up in an asylum, asserting: "I have never believed in madness as a disease, only in feeble-mindedness" (49, 172).

[21]Roth, "Eismeer des Schweigens. Ernst Herbeck: 'Alexander' — Ausgewählte Texte 1961-1981" [Polar Sea of Silence. Ernst Herbeck: 'Alexander.' Selected Texts 1961-1981], *Die Zeit* 14 Jan. 1983: 36.

[22]"Das allmähliche Verstummen der Sprache," p. 68.

[23]On the "deconstructive" intent of these passages see Walter Grond, "Gerhard Roths *Landläufiger Tod*. Zur Genese eines Romans"; W. G. Sebald, "In einer wildfremden Gegend. Zu Gerhard Roths Roman *Landläufiger Tod*," *manuskripte: Zeitschrift für Literatur* 26.92 (1986): 52-56; and Walter Hinck, "Die aus den Fugen geratene Welt des Dorfes.

Roth's fascination with this "wondrous" language is associated with his belief that the public sphere has completely disintegrated. If, as he suggests, all language and thought are part of a system of falsifications and deceptions, the only solution is to discover a new, purified form of discourse that is not yet contaminated by social usage. This leads him away from the social world to the realm of mysticism, madness, and fantasy. Like the language of mysticism and madness, literature, too, he suggests, can reveal a reality that would otherwise remain hidden:

> Literature is also a linguistic religion. Language has a metaphysical aura; it can think and speak itself. It forms connections *organically*; like Münchhausen, it can pull itself by its own hair out of contradictions. In this condition, language is a drug for the writer and can be one for the reader. It disembodies itself. The words are electrical charges; for the briefest moments, the brightness of their flashes tears the landscape away from the language of darkness. There is a *transformation* of language [*Umsprachung* der Sprache]. Humanity [Menschheit] is language [Sprachheit]; language is inner life. (One does not lie before it as usual like a kicking beetle trapped on its back).[24]

Roth describes an unmediated mode of discourse in which language coincides with things; language is no longer a system of signs that refer to things in the real world, but an entity with a "metaphysical aura" that "speaks" and "thinks" itself. Humanity *is* language; language *is* inner life, the neologism *Sprachheit* serving to underscore its identity with *Menschheit*. Unlike the language of the everyday world, this language will magically dissolve contradictions, providing clarity and insight into the nature of things instead of leaving one helpless and confused before its ambiguities like the kicking beetle trapped on its back. By contributing to this linguistic transformation, literature, Roth implies, can purify language and thereby help to make possible a discourse free of ideological domination.

The gulf between such ideas and the everyday world portrayed in Roth's essays and fiction is indicative both of the uncompromising nature of his project as well as of its ultimate futility.[25] On the one side, he describes an impenetrable world dominated by an alien ideology, unauthentic meanings, and Kuhnian incommensu-

---

Landläufiger Tod — Gerhard Roths Roman und seine Chronik," Frankfurter Allgemeine Zeitung 20 Nov. 1984: B3.

[24]"Das allmähliche Verstummen der Sprache," p. 68.

[25]This gulf is apparent, for example, in those fantastic sections of *Landläufiger Tod* described above. They are as strangely irrelevant to the everyday world inhabited by the other figures in the novel as they are to the world inhabited by the reader, the most tolerant of whom might be excused for losing patience with nearly fifty pages of disconnected sentences. These passages have also been widely criticized by reviewers. See for example Fritz J. Raddatz, "Epische Geisterbahn. Gerhard Roths *Landläufiger Tod* und *Dorfchronik* zu diesem Buch," *Die Zeit* 9 Nov. 1984, who describes them as "'overwritten' — and falling apart," and "world-less" ["weltlos"], and Peter Laemmle, "Die Suche nach der verlorenen Universalität. Gedanken zu Gerhard Roths epischem Großversuch *Landläufiger Tod*," *Süddeutsche Zeitung* 23 Feb. 1985, who characterizes them as "filler."

rability; on the other, he posits a world of clarity, truth, and light. But there seems to be nothing in-between. Human existence, however, plays itself out in the ambiguous regions between these two poles. It is here, in the social world of communicative interaction, that the struggle for truth, justice, and meaning takes place, but Roth seems to have little interest in this deliberate and often frustrating process. "I desire a land in which a justice system is superfluous, even if that is a utopia," he said in an interview a few years ago.[26] A world with no need for a justice system would be a world without human beings; "utopia," it should be recalled, means "Land of Nowhere."

Roth has expressed surprise that critics have judged his works by the standards of realism and have often hesitated to follow him into the imaginary realm he has constructed.[27] But the reason for this hesitancy is clear: the problems implied in Roth's work have implications for the real world. The province of literature does, of course, include the irrational, the unconscious, and the fantastic, but even these elements are extrapolations of reality and can be understood only in relation to it. As Gerald Graff has expressed it: "Whether fantasy makes us more critical or merely more solipsistic and self-indulgent depends finally on whether it is account-able to something that is not fantasy."[28] In Roth's work, imaginative elements are embedded in a world we clearly recognize as our own. To deny the relationship between the real and the imaginary is to see literature as an empty diversion, and in the final analysis as irrelevant.

[26]"Ich wünsche mir ein Land, in dem die Justiz überflüssig ist, auch wenn das eine Utopie ist." "Die Fürchterlichsten sind die Gebildeten." Interview with Ditta Rudle, *Wochenpresse* (Vienna) 17 July 1987: 39.

[27]In a conversation with Peter Laemmle. See his "Eintreten in die eigene Besessenheit. Gerhard Roths Prosaband *Der Untersuchungsrichter*," *Süddeutsche Zeitung* 17 Sept. 1988.

[28]Gerald Graff, *Literature against Itself: Literary Ideas in Modern Society* (Chicago: University of Chicago Press, 1979), p. 100. Cf. also Fritz J. Raddatz: "Certainly, art has something to do with the irrational or with the unconscious; but even Freud saw its greatness in the fact that it opened up an horizon of hope. Gerhard Roth varies Freud's themes of erotic violence and the death instinct — but he does not provide what Freud demanded: the attempt, by writing, to lend concrete form to the hope for a reasonable society." "Epische Geisterbahn," p. 2.

5 Mesmerism and the Transformation of the Public Sphere: Peter Sloterdijk's *Der Zauberbaum*

DER ZAUBERBAUM [THE MAGIC TREE] (1985) is Peter Sloterdijk's (b. 1947) only work of fiction to date. The novel, which bears the subtitle *Die Entstehung der Psychoanalyse im Jahr 1785. Ein epischer Versuch zur Philosophie der Psychologie* [The Origin of Psychoanalysis in the Year 1785. An Epic Essay on the Philosophy of Psychology], spans the period from 1785 to well into the first half of the twentieth century. The protagonist, Jan van Leyden, a recently graduated medical student, is described as "a younger brother of that psychologist who at the turn of the nineteenth and twentieth centuries developed a new language for the psyche [Seele]."[1] Like Freud after him, van Leyden embarks for France to study psychology, which was strongly influenced at the time by the theories of Anton Mesmer and his pupil the Marquis de Puységur, who introduced hypnosis as a therapeutic technique into psychology. In the course of the novel, van Leyden travels to Strassburg, to Paris, and finally to the town of Buzancy, where Puységur, "magnetized" his patients by connecting them with lines to an elm tree, the "magic tree" of the title, to allow the healing "fluid" to pass through them.[2] After numerous adventures, including stimulating visits to Parisian salons, erotic encounters, an Oedipal dream, and a narrow escape from the guillotine, Jan van Leyden returns to Berggasse 19, where his character merges with that of the aging Sigmund Freud. The connection to psychoanalysis promised by the title is thus established.

[1]*Der Zauberbaum: Die Entstehung der Psychoanalyse im Jahr 1785. Ein epischer Versuch zur Philosophie der Psychologie* (Frankfurt: Suhrkamp, 1985), p. 15. Unless otherwise indicated, all translations throughout are my own. Further references to *Der Zauberbaum* will be indicated parenthetically in the text.

[2]This account of the Marquis de Puységur's treatments is based on historical fact. Mesmer also employed magnetized trees as part of his treatments. See Robert Darnton, *Mesmerism and the End of the Enlightenment in France* (Cambridge: Harvard University Press, 1968), pp. 8, 58. Sloterdijk refers to this book in *Der Zauberbaum*, p. 25.

But this is less a work about the origins of psychoanalysis and modern psychology than it is a *Bildungsroman* chronicling the protagonist's "education" from the scientific rationalism of the Enlightenment to a new, post-rational philosophical position. This philosophical development is Sloterdijk's main concern. Hence, the narrator declares that despite the historical characters and milieu this is not an historical novel. Its subject matter, he says, is "the pure present and nothing but the present." Like most of Sloterdijk's other, non-fictional works, *Der Zauberbaum* is about the modern world. It takes place, the narrator continues, "in the expanded Now that we call modernity" (15).

Why then did Sloterdijk set the novel in pre-revolutionary France? He clearly was drawn to France in the 1780s because of parallels between that decade and our own time. Both periods are dominated by rationalism, a preoccupation with science, and, perhaps as a reaction, a simultaneous fascination with irrational forces that promise to restore the harmony and synthesis that cold rationalism has allegedly destroyed.[3] The triumph of instrumental reason was embodied in the lethal efficiency of the guillotine. Mesmerism, by contrast, posited the existence of a universal fluid that had the power to restore individuals to health and re-establish the harmony of man with nature.[4] The connection between personal health and the possibility of transforming society was responsible for the radical utopian undercurrent in some forms of Mesmerism. It was thought by some that a change in the physical constitution could have moral and political consequences. Nicolas Bergasse, for example, believed that the "peaceful flow of the fluid would produce a blissfully healthy, happy, and justly organized France."[5] Although it originally began as an outgrowth of the Enlightenment, Mesmerism eventually developed into a kind of spiritualism. It offered its adherents "a new faith, a faith that marked the end of the Enlightenment, the advent of the Revolution, and the dawning of the nineteenth century."[6]

Mesmerism promised to heal the division between mind and body, subject and object, posited by Cartesian rationalism. It thus prefigured what Sloterdijk sees as one of his own goals: to transform the public sphere by articulating new public meanings to replace the unauthentic ones of the dominant ideology. For Sloterdijk, the source of these unauthentic meanings is a persistent Cartesianism that has led to the aggrandizement of the subject. Modernity, he claims, is subjectivity gone wild. "Is a certain self-becoming [Ichwerdung] in its essence perhaps just as

---

[3]Robert Darnton points out that France of the 1780s was characterized by a "boundless faith in science" (32), but also that "the literate French of the late 1780s tended to reject the cold rationalism of the midcentury in favor of a more exotic intellectual diet. They yearned for the supra-rational and the scientifically mysterious. They buried Voltaire and flocked to Mesmer" (165).

[4]See Darnton, esp. chapter 1.

[5]Darnton, p. 114.

[6]Darnton, p. 165.

catastrophic as a reactor explosion?" he asks.[7] Our "self-desirousness" ["Selbstge-wolltheit"] has transformed modernity, as it had for Novalis two hundred years earlier, into a "self-grinding mill" propelled by rationality, science, and the belief in progress.[8] Its chief characteristic is blind mobility, or "mobilization," a term Sloterdijk prefers because it suggests "the kernel of violence in key scientific, military, and industrial processes."[9] "Modernity is ontologically pure Being-as-Movement [Sein-zur Bewegung]," he maintains; but this "kinetic utopia" has disintegrated, leaving us to confront the prospect of "an uncontrollable, catastrophic heteromobility."[10] What is needed, Sloterdijk claims, is "an alteration of our sense of 'Being'" that would dethrone the subject and allow for the articulation of new public meanings.[11] Such meanings, he hopes, would overcome the dichotomy of subject and object and help to restore our primary relationship to the biosphere. They would enable us to see the world not as an obsessive mobility but as a "symphonic process."[12]

By positing the existence of forces not immediately accessible to the observing and thinking subject, Mesmerism presented an early challenge to Cartesianism. In his *Critique of Cynical Reason*, Sloterdijk credits it with "the real discovery of the unconscious." The birth year of "Enlightenment depth psychology," he maintains, was 1784, when the Marquis de Puységur discovered hypnosis and experienced the strange rapport between doctor and patient that later, under the name "trans-

---

[7]Sloterdijk, *Eurotaoismus: Zur Kritik der politischen Kinetik* [Euro-Taoism: Toward a Critique of Political Kinetics] (Frankfurt: Suhrkamp, 1989), p. 120.

[8]*Eurotaoismus*, pp. 37, 41. In his 1799 essay "Die Christenheit oder Europa" [Christianity or Europe], Novalis described his own society, which was dominated by the ideas of the Enlightenment, as "eine sich selbst mahlende Mühle."

[9]*Eurotaoismus*, p. 52.

[10]*Eurotaoismus*, pp. 24, 37.

[11]*Eurotaoismus*, p. 200.

[12]Sloterdijk, *Critique of Cynical Reason*, trans. Michael Eldred, Theory and History of Literature 40 (Minneapolis: University of Minnesota Press, 1987), p. 542; *Kritik der zynischen Vernunft*, 2 vols. (Frankfurt: Suhrkamp, 1983), 2: 943. Sloterdijk's ideas show the strong influence of Martin Heidegger, who maintained that philosophy has been transformed into "the empirical science of man." He speculates on the possibility of "a thinking which is more sober-minded than the incessant frenzy of rationalization and the intoxicating quality of cybernetics." See Heidegger, "The End of Philosophy and the Task of Thinking," in *Basic Writings*, ed. David Farrell Krell (New York: Harper and Row, 1977), pp. 376, 391. See also, in the same volume, "Being and Time: Introduction" and "The Question Concerning Technology." Sloterdijk discusses Heidegger in *Critique of Cynical Reason*, pp. 195-210; *Kritik der zynischen Vernunft*, 1: 369-96.

ference," became an important element of Freudian therapy.[13] But the discovery of hypnosis was important not only for psychology; it also had far-reaching philosophical implications, for it documented the untenability of what Sloterdijk calls the "transparency illusion":

> All this says that at least since the late eighteenth century, the illusion of a transparent human self-consciousness has been systematically destroyed. Somnabulant phenomena provide provocative proofs that consciousness does not know everything about itself. In the state of magnetic lucidity, a zone of knowledge speaks that remains inaccessible to surface consciousness.[14]

This development marked the end of the "objective" vision of the world. It now became necessary to focus on the "glasses" through which the world was seen; the rational apparatus itself became problematic.[15]

In *Der Zauberbaum*, Mesmerism is the intellectual hub around which Sloterdijk spins an entertaining story about a young man's search for knowledge, identity, and meaning in pre-revolutionary France.[16] Van Leyden begins as a naive young scientist with a superior air of skepticism toward all phenomena beyond the grasp of enlightened reason. He adopted this skepticism from his teacher, a former Jesuit who seemed "to parody his frustrated Catholicism with cynical language games" and who acquainted van Leyden with "the basic principle of the Austrian philosophy of life," that is, "with a serious frivolousness or better frivolous seriousness from which the wilted mind wanders in every direction until everything is imaginable but nothing has any validity" (24). Van Leyden's teacher exemplifies what Sloterdijk refers to as "cynical reason," which he defines as "enlightened

---

[13]Sloterdijk, *Critique of Cynical Reason*, pp. 47, 49; *Kritik der zynischen Vernunft*, 1: 108, 111.

[14]*Critique of Cynical Reason*, p. 49; *Kritik der zynischen Vernunft*, 1: 111. He continues a few pages later: "If every ego is underlaid by an unconscious, then that is the end of the self-satisfaction of a consciousness that thinks it knows itself, and thus knows how to value itself." *Critique*, p. 50; *Kritik*, 1: 113. "Transparency illusion" is, of course, Sloterdijk's term for the phenomenon discussed in chapter 3 as the "transparency thesis" and as the metaphor of the mind as a mirror. This is the notion that there exists an uncomplicated relationship between subject and object, that, as Joseph Margolis put it, the world is "cognitively transparent to the mind." See Joseph Margolis, *Pragmatism without Foundations: Reconciling Realism and Relativism* (Oxford: Basil Blackwell, 1986), p. xvi. See also Richard Rorty, *Philosophy and the Mirror of Nature* (Princeton: Princeton University Press, 1979).

[15]*Critique of Cynical Reason*, p. 59; *Kritik der zynischen Vernunft*, 1: 130.

[16]One is inclined to agree with Anton Krättli that Sloterdijk seems "predestined to be a novelist" and that in *Der Zauberbaum* he is "entirely himself, showing his true talents." Krättli, "Transplantationen der Vergangenheit. *Der Zauberbaum*. Zu einem epischen Versuch von Peter Sloterdijk," *Schweizer Monatshefte* 65 (1985): 427.

false consciousness."[17] This glib, superficial rationality is repeatedly challenged during van Leyden's educational journey through France. It is shaken first by his Strassburg mentor Dr. LeBrasseur, who confronts him with the inevitable fact of decay and death and reminds him that science is based on research, research on facts, and facts on corpses. Van Leyden begins to lose "the secure ground beneath his feet"; in Austria, one never enunciated such "hard truths" (42, 44). The most important lesson van Leyden learns from LeBrasseur is contained in the chapter entitled "Noch etwas — die Türme und das moderne Ich betreffend" [One More Thing — Concerning Towers and the Modern Ego], in which LeBrasseur takes his pupil to the top of the high tower of the Strassburg cathedral, whence he delivers a lengthy and somewhat quixotic lecture on subjectivity.

Throughout his writing, Sloterdijk frequently uses the image of the tower, construction metaphors, and the idea of verticality or height to illustrate the self-deceptive search for power and metaphysical security that he sees at the core of subjectivity:

> Setting up principles [prinzipielle Aufstellung] is the action-lie of the active subject, which at the climax of its development covers the earth with unstable structures. In these structures it is not the tendency to verticality that is wrong...The sham originates in the pose of certainty, which attempts to provide an uncertain life with its own firm base on indestructible foundations.[18]

In order to buttress these structures, Western man employs rationality, science, and the notion of objective truth. But, according to Sloterdijk, these too are illusions, engaged by the subject to maintain the delusion of cognitive autonomy and to help it avoid confronting "the unavoidable," the question of a deeper meaning and reality:

> What we know as rationality is a way of dealing with 'reality' that is only possible as a consequence of the mind's initial and indispensable evasion of incommensurable forces. It is an approach that orients itself towards what is bearable, imaginable, clear, accessible. The accessible [das Umgängliche] results from our necessary avoidance of the unavoidable [Umgehen des Unumgänglichen]. This avoidance, as an evasion of what is all too weighty, is the basic effort at the center of all subjectivities.[19]

---

[17]Knowledge is bound up with power, he writes, and thinking has become little more than a strategy in the service of self-preservation. Sloterdijk, *Critique of Cynical Reason*, p. 5; *Kritik der zynischen Vernunft*, 1: 8; 10-12; 37.

[18]*Eurotaoismus*, p. 326. Cf. Heidegger's essay "Building Dwelling Thinking," in which, in a somewhat different context, he calls attention to the etymological connection between *bauen* and *(ich) bin*. *Basic Writings*, p. 325.

[19]*Eurotaoismus*, pp. 261-62.

The quest for knowledge is driven not by the desire for "enlightenment" but by the need for "alleviations."[20] Truth is not "correspondence with the facts" but the product of a culturally determined notion of correctness, a convenient and useful foundation for the edifice of subjectivity. The subject is a fiction, a web of lies.[21]

Ideas of this kind are behind LeBrasseur's observation that every tower contains the story of the origin of the modern ego. Medicine, if it is to be successful, must deal with the question of subjectivity; it must begin with what LeBrasseur terms "an awakening to the psychology of height":

> It is not a matter of this or that illness but of the principle of illness itself. It is a question of the cleavage that goes through the lives of tower-building subjects. Whoever builds upwards in this way has a problem with the ground. Whoever climbs to such heights sees angry mother earth gaping before him as a horrifying abyss. Height symptoms, nothing but height symptoms — that is what we are dealing with (54).

The underlying problem is thus not a medical one, but a philosophical one; it is a matter not of the disease that modern human beings have, LeBrasseur continues, but of the disease that they are (55). In search of power and epistemic certainty, these "tower-building subjects" have alienated themselves from the earth and from life itself.[22] Mesmerism can heal this psychological-philosophical disease, LeBrasseur tells his pupil, for it views the individual not as an isolated being, but as a particle in the universal fluid that unites all things. Moreover, by healing the division in the individual, it also promises to heal the divisions in society. The private and the public spheres are thus intimately interconnected. "For that reason, when seen in terms of the fluid, health and freedom are two sides of the same coin" (58), LeBrasseur concludes.

Van Leyden's encounter with LeBrasseur as well as his own psychological discoveries lead him to question the traditional notion of subjectivity. The most important of these discoveries is the influence of unconscious processes on human thought and behavior. When he observes the rehearsal of a traveling acting troop, van Leyden is astonished when a young actress unwittingly deviates from the written text and seems to perform a role from deep within her psyche. The ego, van Leyden concludes, has a number of "hidden whisperers, commentators, seducers, commanders, and accomplices." And what is the soul, he asks, but "the

---

[20]*Eurotaoismus*, p. 260.

[21]"So at the end of its work the subject becomes transparent as an insupportable and at the same time insoluble fiction — some say a divine pack of lies." *Eurotaoismus*, p. 204. On the question of truth see *Eurotaoismus*, pp. 243-46; 321.

[22]Sloterdijk sees connections among the quest for power, the need for metaphysical security, and the fear of falling: "Where power rises for the first time to dizzying heights, people, both the powerful and the victims, begin to have experiences with a new quality of riskiness. For this reason, the state, metaphysics, and fear of falling are entities of equal age." *Eurotaoismus*, p. 322.

permanent conversation that our ego engages in with its companions?" (116). As a result of these insights, van Leyden claims that he no longer knows what he means when he says "I"; psychology has become impossible, he says, because its basic premise, the notion of a consistent individual identity, is no longer valid (139). The discovery of this inner "demonology" (116), which he later calls "the Unconscious" (186), leads to the collapse of the "transparency illusion." The "highly praised simplicity and transparency of consciousness" (186) are gone forever. And so are the notion of science as a privileged mode of inquiry and the possibility of objective knowledge. When he meets the Marquis de Puységur, van Leyden realizes for the first time

> that research could be the greatest of all life's lies, because it was based on the hypothesis that through the collecting of so-called experiences an individual could remain the same person he feels himself to be in his seeking and thinking (249).

Research is also a "lie" because it equates knowledge and truth with the accumulation of facts and epitomizes the adversarial approach to the world that Sloterdijk regards as essential to modern rationality and science. "Research...accepts the intellectual and practical duel with Being [dem Seienden]...In research, the spirit of subjectivity appears as though concentrated in an endless project."[23] In science, Sloterdijk maintains, the ruthlessness of subjectivity reaches its apex. Scientific method demonstrates the war of the subject against the object, for the natural sciences derive their methods from military thinking. The will to know, he writes, implies the arming of the subject against the object; objective knowledge has the characteristics of a weapon. Modern science can only be described "as a war of exploitation and annihilation [waged by] advanced civilization against the biosphere."[24] Science, research, objective knowledge, rationality, progress, the facts — these are the key elements of that predatory epistemology that for Sloterdijk forms the foundation of the tower of subjectivity. His views, like those of Gerhard Roth, recall Feyerabend's claim that "rational" is merely a word "which can be connected with almost any idea of procedure" and Habermas's and Aronowitz's assertions that science is determined by a cognitive interest in domination and control.[25]

In *Der Zauberbaum*, this ruthless epistemology is exemplified by the director of the Salpêtrière, Monsieur Merri, who orients himself toward the "hard facts" of reality and claims to know his place in the order of things (140). Merri is an example of the tower-building subject who constructs his edifice on supposed knowledge of the truth; this knowledge then becomes the "weapon" he uses in a

---

[23]Sloterdijk, *Kopernikanische Mobilmachung und ptolemäische Abrüstung* [Copernican Mobilization and Ptolemaic Disarmament] (Frankfurt: Suhrkamp, 1987), pp. 106-07.

[24]*Critique of Cynical Reason*, pp. 349-50; *Kritik der zynischen Vernunft*, 2: 640-41.

[25]Paul Feyerabend, *Farewell to Reason* (London: Verso, 1987), p. 10. See also the introduction to this book.

war against the object, in this case his fellow human beings. As if they were indifferent things, the patients in his hospital are arranged "systematically" according to their afflictions. He even hopes that those with terminal illnesses can be brought together in a "meaningful concentration" so that the inconveniences associated with death can be confined to one location (196). The enemy, he says, is the human body, which must be subjected to the dictates of reason:

> We have done much to get the body under control. For indeed, bodies, above all, are our enemies. They are full of unpredictable outbreaks against reason and order. They are over-flowing with abnormal growths and senseless incursions against the world and themselves...(197).

Toward the end of the novel, Merri achieves the final victory of reason and technology over the body as he presides over the efficient operation of the guillotine, which he praises as "a triumph of organization" and "the first alliance of gravity, thermodynamics, and patriotism" (307). There is no inner life, he tells van Leyden, and now that the facts have been discovered, there is no need for psychology. "Now the facts count once more. How many divisions has the unconscious, Monsieur?" (309).[26]

Knowledge of the facts also forms the basis of the idea of progress, a key concept of Enlightenment thinking; but like science, it too implies the subjugation of nature. Monsieur Boisdeffre claims that the universe is being "alphabetically" organized and compares Paris to Sparta and Rome (142-43). Similarly, Condorcet, the discoverer of the "law of unstoppable progress" (215), believes that a "new nature," directed and created by man, must inevitably lead to new results. "We control what we have ourselves brought forth" (206), he insists. And Merri declares before the guillotine: "We are making progress" (307). But according to Dr. Marat and the Abbé Galiani, who visit the Salpêtrière with van Leyden, this notion of progress is based on an optical illusion. Marat describes Merri as a partially blind man who does not recognize the limits of his vision and who quickly destroys everything that does not fit into his limited perspective (204). The Abbé Galiani depicts Condorcet as a rider in a vehicle loaded with "a thousand barrels of the most hopeful illusions." But because he is himself a passenger, Condorcet is unable to maintain an objective perspective on his progress. If he could observe himself from without, he would see that his world voyage took place in a glass of water (208-09).

Marat and the abbé attack the pivotal idea of the supporters of progress that reality can be deciphered and that the future is open. The accumulation of facts, Galiani implies, does not lead to progress because it does not lead to insights into a deeper meaning. "Analysis, enlightenment, science — simply attempts to provide

---

[26]The notion of instrumental reason as the principle enabling violence against the body suggests the influence of both Adorno and Foucault on Sloterdijk. See Axel Honneth, "Foucault und Adorno. Zwei Formen einer Kritik der Moderne," in *"Postmoderne" oder der Kampf um die Zukunft: Die Kontroverse in Wissenschaft, Kunst und Gesellschaft*, ed. Peter Kemper (Frankfurt: Fischer, 1988), pp. 127-44.

the old incomprehension with a new framework" (206), he declares. Galiani suggests that empirical knowledge and science are a way of dealing with reality that enables us to avoid confronting the basic unanswerable questions, what Sloterdijk referred to in the quotation above as "the unavoidable." They do not bring us closer to the truth; they merely create the illusion of certainty and thus support the edifice of subjectivity.

The shakiness of this edifice is graphically illustrated by the patient in the Salpêtrière who believes he is Louis XV. Although the patient's world is based on a premise that others regard as objectively wrong, he is none the worse for living in his own subjective world. In the final analysis, the facts are irrelevant, as the "king" himself points out: "Science is condemned to empiricism, and empiricism plays itself out down below, near the objects. It can never know anything about what is above" (220). Determining what constitutes "objective reality" cannot provide a secure frame of reference or any guarantees for truth. It can merely provide a pretext for the subject's campaign against the Other. In the name of reality, Merri also murders his unfortunate patient, whose existence is inconsistent with his doctor's perception of the facts.

Within a world preoccupied with science, rationality, and the violent triumph of the facts, Mesmerism promises an oasis of harmony. Mesmerism seems to have recognized subjectivity and the antagonism between subject and object as the cause of society's malady. The Marquis de Puységur tells van Leyden that many people are unhappy because they continue to see themselves as "autonomous critical subjects, little kings, as it were, who reside in the middle of their world and must oversee and rule everything" (254). This subjectivity [Mittelpunktich], he says, is the principle of stagnation that prevents the individual from establishing the desired contact with the Other. Animal magnetism, by contrast, is founded on "trust in the healing power of community" (251); it is "nothing other than a very deep healing communion" (252) that requires "self-abandon" ["Hingabe"] (255) from its adherents. In his elm tree therapy, the Marquis employs a form of hypnosis to help his patients resolve unconscious conflicts, but he attributes these "cures" to the flow of the magnetic fluid. The guiding principles of animal magnetism, he says, are "faith and desire" (251). Van Leyden immediately reacts to the nebulousness of these ideas, which, he recognizes, can easily be abused. The Marquis responds that van Leyden's skepticism comes from the mistrust human beings have for one another in a world governed by the principle *homo homini lupus*. Animal magnetism, however, belongs to a different world, and those who choose to acknowledge its insights must simply "decide" to go in a different direction (251-52). Puységur's ideas, a combination of spiritualism and pseudo-science, seem to be predicated on nothing more than a desire to be healthy and to live in a better world, and van Leyden admits that he has difficulty applying them to himself. Instead of a psychological theory, the Marquis seems to be advocating a new religion.

Rather than the final goal, Mesmerism is merely one stop in van Leyden's intellectual journey. Before going to his own session with Puységur, he formulates a "Tractatus psychologicus-philosophicus," which incorporates the utopian ideals of Mesmerism and restates its tenets in philosophical terms. As in Mesmerism, the main focus of van Leyden's critique is the "tower-building subject" who seeks objective knowledge as a foundation for certainty and power: "It was important to put an end to the height fantasies of the will to know. One had to perish as a researcher and accept a knowledge that does not give power but understanding" (280). Van Leyden replaces subjectivity's architectural metaphors with one that emphasizes the fundamental uncertainty of a life without guarantees. Every human being, he says, is like a "thinking meteorite" (282) that glows when it comes in contact with reality. Glowing means having the possibility to feel one's existence. It therefore makes no sense to seek a foundation or basis for this glowing or to attempt to place oneself above or beyond it. "Meteors know no stopping point and find no certainty in the representation [Vorstellen] of the world" (283). In its quest for "scientific certainty," modern philosophy has forgotten the principle of glowing. Van Leyden traces the source of this philosophical difficulty to Descartes, who posited the *cogito sum* as a foundation for knowledge, thereby introducing subjectivity into philosophy and paving the way for psychology.[27] Psychology must do penance for the "Saying-I-Am"; it is, van Leyden maintains, our "philosophie maudite": "The more that human beings arm themselves with an 'I think' from the armory of modern ideologies, the more psychology will arise in this society to regulate the ghosts" (284).

Rather than a new science, psychology is an attempt to cure the disease of modern philosophy, which in its obsession with subjectivity has neglected its higher purpose: to create "new fusions" (285) and new possibilities for synthesis. By assuming this philosophical task, a future psychology could accomplish what Mesmerism could only hope for. If it could dissolve "the central illusion of an ego" (290), it could re-establish the harmonious relationship between subject and object and prepare the way for the community envisioned by the Mesmerists. "When the subject [das Ich] dissolves itself, its life is transformed from the limiting Over and Against to a limitless In and With" (291). This future psychology, which would lead humanity "beyond its biological-social conception," contains within it "the utopia of real freedom" (290). By healing the divided subject, it could prepare the way for "a whole of a higher order" (291).

The creation of "new fusions" and of "a whole of a higher order" is an important theme in some of Sloterdijk's essays. In his *Kopernikanische Mobil-*

---

[27]Cf. also Michel Foucault's critique of the *cogito*. He maintains that
the *cogito* does not lead to an affirmation of being, but it does lead to a whole series of questions concerned with being: What must I be, I who think and who am my thought, in order to be what I do not think, in order for my thought to be what I am not? What is this being, then, that shimmers and, as it were, glitters in the opening of the *cogito*, yet is not sovereignly given in it or by it? What, then, is the connection, the difficult link, between being and thought?
The Order of Things: An Archaeology of the Human Sciences (1966; New York: Random House, 1970), p. 325.

machung und ptolemäische Abrüstung [Copernican Mobilization and Ptolemaic Disarmament], for example, he claims that what is needed is "neo-synthetic thinking," such as that contained in Joachim Ernst Berendt's *Nada Brahma: Die Welt ist Klang* [Nada Brahma: The World is Sound].[28] Berendt's "musical-ontological New Synthesis," he writes, promises to solve a problem that has mystified the greatest thinkers, for in a naive and unpretentious way it achieves

> the complete mediation of subject and object, the definitive abolition [Aufhebung] of the opposition between interior and exterior, the peaceful dissolving of the subject in substance, the inspired evaporation of substance in the subject.[29]

Although he is critical of the totalizing, utopian aspects of Berendt's book and characterizes his discussion of it as an "intellectual experiment," Sloterdijk cannot disguise his fascination for some of Berendt's ideas,[30] which bear some similarity to those of the Mesmerists. What Anton Mesmer and his followers attempted in the eighteenth century, Berendt attempts in the twentieth: to re-establish the "universal harmony" of all things. The reason for Sloterdijk's interest in both theories, as fanciful and ultimately untenable as they might be, is clear. Both are attempts to discover alternative modes of Being and thus to formulate *new public meanings* to replace the dominant ideology, which, Sloterdijk claims, is determined by an adversarial relationship between subject and object as manifested in a culture dominated by rationality and science.

What unites van Leyden's and Sloterdijk's views with those of the Mesmerists is the belief that *santé* and *liberté*, the private and the public spheres, are intimately connected. For van Leyden, the utopia of real freedom can only be realized as the result of a psychological-philosophical revolution in every person. This idea manifests itself throughout the novel in the use of psychological and philosophical vocabulary to describe political events, and vice versa. Towards the beginning of the book, for example, the narrator notes that the bourgeois revolution took place just a few years "after the Bastille of the unconscious had been stormed" and that the revolution seemed to many "a thoroughgoing political therapy" (18). And when the new republic defends itself against counter-revolutionaries, he describes its actions in psychological terms: "Shaken by the fever of self-assertion, [the republic] had lost the ability to differentiate and begun to destroy everything which it did not want to believe was part of itself" (305). Finally, when writing about the wars spawned by the French Revolution, the narrator sums up this idea when he

---

[28]*Kopernikanische Mobilmachung*, p. 101.

[29]*Kopernikanische Mobilmachung*, pp. 103-04; 117. One of Berendt's goals, Sloterdijk maintains, is "to 'ground' ['erden'] subjectivity ontologically" (102).

[30]Berendt's main thesis is that "the world is sound." What he offers, according to Sloterdijk, is "a kind of free-jazz cosmology on the basis of theorems from the physics of sound and crisis diagnoses in the style of *New Age* publishing, which is no longer only American, surrounded by Tibetan Om chanting, the new European critique of reason, particle research, paleolinguistics, and Zen-Buddhism." *Kopernikanische Mobilmachung*, p. 85.

asks: "Did those who danced around the tree of liberty understand that such dances undeniably become dances of death as long as the tree of liberty is not identical with the tree of self-knowledge?" (310). Freedom and self-knowledge are co-extensive, and the former, the novel implies, can be achieved only on the basis of the latter.

The notion that historical and political events are a manifestation of philosophical or psychological conflicts also permeates Sloterdijk's essays. The problem of the accumulation of capital in Marxist theory, he writes, can actually be traced back to an original "accumulation of subjectivity." The dynamic of capitalism is carried by "structures of self-actualization and self-intensification" that preceded and determined economic developments.[31] Similarly, he maintains, the "disunion" ["Zerrissenheit"][32] of modernity mirrors the division in the modern ego. Liberal democracy has failed, he claims, because it has not been able to deal with this underlying philosophical-psychological problem. Instead, its goal has been the "neutralization of what is existentially most important"; it has replaced "existential passions" with "practical 'interests.'" There is a "credibility gap" not because politics has lost touch with the true concerns of the people, but because the people are "alienated" from their "passions." As a result, the democratic process has become a meaningless ritual.[33] "In many places, democracy seems to be merely a cover name for the modernization of impotence," he writes.[34] After the "subtraction of their passions," people remain "hollow bodies" who can participate in politics only with a feeble voice or — a play on the double meaning of *Stimme* — with a meaningless vote:

> Not without reason do we call what remains after the abstraction of what is most important 'the vote' ['die Stimme']. Whoever has gone through the process of politicization retains only his or her vote [Stimme], with which nothing can be expressed of the abundance and the pain of life.[35]

Sloterdijk is reacting here to what Habermas has called the "refeudalization" of the public sphere, its transformation from a place where fundamental existential issues could be discussed in an atmosphere free of domination into a forum for the competition of private interests.[36] As a result of this development, Sloterdijk is

---

[31]*Eurotaoismus*, pp. 61, 64.

[32]*Critique of Cynical Reason*, p. 541; *Kritik der zynischen Vernunft*, 2: 942.

[33]See *Eurotaoismus*, pp. 223-26.

[34]*Kopernikanische Mobilmachung*, pp. 66-67.

[35]*Eurotaoismus*, p. 228.

[36]Jürgen Habermas, "The Public Sphere: An Encyclopedia Article (1964)," trans. Sara Lennox and Frank Lennox, *New German Critique* 1.3 (1974): 54. (Originally published in *Fischer Lexikon: Staat und Politik* [Frankfurt: Fischer, 1964], pp. 220-26). See also

deeply cynical about discourse itself. He rejects the idea of consensus as a realizable possibility as well as the Habermasian notion of an "ideal speech situation" in which consensus is anticipated counterfactually. "It is tempting to poke fun at the 'methodological antirealism' of the dialogue idea...To preserve the healing fiction of a free dialogue is one of the last tasks of philosophy."[37] For Sloterdijk, there can be no discourse oriented toward reaching understanding, no communicative action; all discourse is strategic. The new public meanings that he advocates cannot be articulated through communication; nor can they be realized through the democratic process. Like van Leyden and the Mesmerists in *Der Zauberbaum*, Sloterdijk suggests that new meanings will emerge and that the public sphere will be transformed only as the result of a psychological or philosophical change within each individual. As the narrator of *Der Zauberbaum* put it, freedom must become identical with self-realization.[38]

Like Gerhard Roth, Sloterdijk implies that the public sphere is so corrupt that communicative action and meaningful political participation are impossible. He therefore turns inward, placing his hopes on the possibility of a personal psychological or philosophical transformation. Throughout his writing there is a disdain not only for discourse and the give-and-take of the political process but also for any outlook that is oriented toward "objective reality" or "the facts," all of which must indeed appear trivial when contrasted with the possibilities of a "new synthesis" and a new mode of Being. But how is this new mode of Being, this new public meaning, to materialize if not as the result of communicative interaction? Sloterdijk's critique of modernity, like Roth's, seems to be propelled as much by a utopian nostalgia for a lost, premodern synthesis and wholeness as by a desire to rectify the excesses of scientific rationality. As Neil Wilson put it in a review of Sloterdijk's *Critique of Cynical Reason*:

> He underscores the death of the Enlightenment by a sentimental and shabby appeal to an all-embracing nostalgia for the mythical womb of pre-Socratic philosophy, glorifies its values to serve as a contrast to the tyranny of our age and gives us new

---

Habermas, *Structural Transformation of the Public Sphere: An Inquiry into a Category of Bourgeois Society*, trans. Thomas Burger and Frederick Lawrence (Cambridge: MIT Press, 1989), esp. section VI.

[37]"Es ist naheliegend, sich über den 'methodischen Antirealismus' der Dialogidee lustig zu machen...Die heilsame Fiktion des freien Dialogs aufrechtzuerhalten, ist eine letzte Aufgabe von Philosophie." Sloterdijk, *Critique of Cynical Reason*, pp. 13-14; *Kritik der zynischen Vernunft*, 1: 50.

[38]Klaus Laermann attributes this tendency to mix individual and social processes to Sloterdijk's refusal to think sociologically: "Since he refuses to think sociologically and, indeed, thinks decidedly antisociologically, Sloterdijk cannot, and does not want to, separate individual from social processes." "Von der Apo zur Apokalypse. Resignation und Fröhliche Wissenschaft am Beispiel von Peter Sloterdijk," in *"Postmoderne" oder Der Kampf um die Zukunft*, p. 221.

hopes and desires to feed on. He offers us a quest-romance that will deliver us from the anxieties of the modern.[39]

The Mesmerists' longing for "universal harmony" finally led them to spiritualism. Sloterdijk's longing for a synthesis of subject and object in what he calls an "ontology of still-being [Noch-Seins]" also has otherworldly overtones. It seems fitting when, on the final page of *Eurotaoismus*, he claims that a real critical theory, his goal, would be identical with mysticism.[40]

---

[39]Neil Wilson, "Punching Out the Enlightenment: A Discussion of Peter Sloterdijk's *Kritik der zynischen Vernunft*," *New German Critique* 41 (1987): 64. He continues a few pages later:

Ignored are the possibilities that bourgeois ideals still serve to justify our actions, scientific knowledge is not always manipulative, justified systems of law and morality still exist...There is an outright dismissal of the traces and existing forms of communicative rationality as false, incomprehensible, inappropriate, corrupt, inadequate and unauthentic. There is a quarrel with *critica* itself; Sloterdijk is looking for the disenchantment of scientific convention and the reenchantment of myth (68).

See also Reinhard Merkel's devastating review of Sloterdijk's *Critique of Cynical Reason*, "Imperiale Gebärde, rasante Gedanken," *Der Spiegel* 37 (13. June 1983): 172-79.

[40]*Eurotaoismus*, pp. 338, 344.

6 The Recovery of the Sacred: Christoph Ransmayr

THE FIRST FULL-LENGTH PUBLICATION of the young Austrian writer Christoph Ransmayr (b. 1954) was the text accompanying a collection of photographs of sunsets. Entitled *Strahlender Untergang: Ein Entwässerungsprojekt oder die Entdeckung des Wesentlichen* [Radiant End: A Drainage Project or the Discovery of the Essential] (1982), Ransmayr's text describes a "scientific" experiment in which a seventy-kilometer square section of the North African desert was transformed into a geometric plane and enclosed by an aluminum wall. Into this terrarium, "which is nothing but the repetition, the imitation of an empty desert," is to be placed "a perhaps forty-year-old man, white, presumably European."[1] In a "Speech before an Academic Delegation" the narrator explains the purpose of the project. Faced with his imminent death in the searing heat, the experimental subject shall be forced, in the final moments of his life, to confront his true self. The book's title thus has a double meaning. "Radiant End" refers not only to the glowing sunsets depicted in the photographs but also to the experimental subject's blistering demise; the "drainage project" refers quite literally to the dehydration of the subject, who is, as the narrator reminds us, seventy percent water; and the discovery of the "essential" is a reference not to a new scientific breakthrough but rather to the subject's discovery of his true identity in the moment of death.[2]

Ransmayr's text, which is aimed at the Western tradition of rationalism and its pursuit of objective knowledge, is a parody of scientific discourse and method. The narrator rejects empirical science and its preoccupation with facts, the accumulation of data, and the construction of systems in favor of what he terms a New Science:

---

[1]All quotations in this paragraph and the next are taken from Ransmayr, *Strahlender Untergang* (Vienna: Christian Brandstätter, 1982). Photographs by Willy Puchner. No page numbers. Unless otherwise indicated, all translations are my own.

[2]Ransmayr's fascination with deserts seems to result from trips to Saudi Arabia and to the American Southwest. Of the latter he has said: "I loved it. I felt again the real weight of things. In the desert you leave everything behind. It is as if you are inside a gigantic watch, and human experience is just a moment." Cited (in English) by Roger Cohen, "Author Updates Ovid Impertinently," *New York Times* 10 May 1990: C20.

The New Science has renounced the transformation of this and all surrounding worlds into an endless collection of objects of observation, definition, imitation, control, and manipulation. It is a science that has turned to the *essential*: to the *desert* and to *disappearance*.

The New Science recognizes humanity's and the world's radical finitude as the one essential fact that traditional science and philosophy (which the narrator describes as "a conglomerate of stupid riddles and questions") have been unable to deal with. Western thought has been "a hard, instrumental thought directed to the quick attainment of ends." This instrumentalism has led not to greater understanding but to Western man's attempts to subjugate the rest of humanity. While destroying everything around him, however, the European has also attempted to extend his own existence into the future. This, the narrator points out, is a contradiction that the desert project is designed to resolve:

Only the New Science can resolve this contradiction by creating the conditions for the disappearance of the Lord of the World....What would be more appropriate than to *dehydrate* a watery creature that has blocked its view of the essential with worthless junk so that it can, after all distractions have been removed, in the rapid course of its demise say *I* for the first time? *I*, and then no more.

Confronted with his own mortality and deprived of the distracting artifacts of civilization his instrumental reason has created, the Lord of the World shall, by saying "I," acknowledge an existential truth about himself that science has merely obscured.[3]

Strahlender Untergang is an attempt to address a fundamental question: What is the meaning of science? Max Weber responded to this same question with a quotation from Tolstoy, who, he says, has given us the simplest answer: "Science is meaningless because it gives no answer to our question, the only question important for us: 'What shall we do and how shall we live?'"[4] In *Strahlender Untergang*, Ransmayr gives a similar response. The book is a critique of a positivistic science that equates knowledge with technological mastery and the accumulation of empirical facts. The New Science is intended to rectify this situation by doing precisely what the old science has failed to do: to re-establish contact with a realm of *ultimate meanings*, to put the Lord of the World in touch once more with the *sacred*. Modern society, Ransmayr implies, cannot meet the human need for transcendent answers and universal meanings. These can be found

---

[3]The book recalls Heidegger's criticism of a technological society in which human beings are estranged from their essential selves: "Meanwhile, man, precisely as the one so threatened, exalts himself to the posture of lord of the earth. In this way the illusion comes to prevail that everything man encounters exists only insofar as it is his construct. This illusion gives rise in turn to one final delusion: it seems as though man everywhere and always encounters only himself." Heidegger, "The Question Concerning Technology," in *Basic Writings*, ed. David Farrell Krell (New York: Harper and Row, 1977), p. 308.

[4]Max Weber, "Science as a Vocation," in *From Max Weber: Essays in Sociology*, trans. H. H. Gerth and C. Wright Mills (Oxford: Oxford University Press, 1946), p. 143.

only *in extremis*, at the margins of the modern world. This marginality is the consequence of life in a technological society that, as Charles Taylor has pointed out, has become "opaque to the sacred":

> The natural environment is seen as transformable matter; but the man-made environment is also without meaning; it is simply the result, or corollary, of the drive for production of individuals and corporations married with the drive of individuals to escape the resulting unlivable environment towards the margins. The fragmentation of community is the stamping out of public meanings. The result is a retreat of faith into a realm of private meanings.[5]

For Taylor, the ideal relationship would be one in which the individual relates to a community as recipient/donor. But this is difficult if not impossible in a society whose public meanings are regarded as alien or unauthentic. Here, identity, like the sacred, can be found only at the margins. According to Peter Berger:

> Institutions cease to be the 'home' of the self; instead they become oppressive realities that distort and estrange the self....Only in the interstitial areas left vacant, as it were, by the institutions (such as the so-called private sphere of social life) can the individual hope to discover or define himself. Identity ceases to be an objectively and subjectively given fact, and instead becomes the goal of an often devious and difficult quest.[6]

This quest — for identity and for the sacred — is the subject of Ransmayr's two novels. In both books, it takes the form of a voyage of discovery to the margins of the civilized world, where the search for empirical knowledge is transformed into a search for existential meaning. Here Ransmayr's protagonists encounter what Sloterdijk referred to in the preceding chapter as "the unavoidable."

The Terrors of Ice and Darkness [*Die Schrecken des Eises und der Finsternis*] (1984) chronicles the 1872-74 Austrian expedition to the North Pole led by Carl Weyprecht and Julius Payer and the (fictional) attempts of a young Italian from Triest, Josef Mazzini, to retrace their steps in 1981. Payer maintains that the expedition's chief goal is "to expand our knowledge," and Weyprecht describes it as "scientific research."[7] Weyprecht's scientific mentor is Isaac Newton, who, he says, derived "the immutable laws on which depend the movements of the stars" from a "simple observation." Newton's accomplishment is for Weyprecht a metaphor for the human ability to solve problems and to progress. He did not

---

[5]Charles Taylor, "From Marxism to the Dialogue Society," in *From Culture to Revolution: The Slant Symposium 1967*, ed. Terry Eagleton and Brian Wicker (London: Sheed and Ward, 1968), p. 166.

[6]Peter Berger, "On the Obsolescence of the Concept of Honour," in *Liberalism and Its Critics*, ed. Michael J. Sandel (New York: New York University Press, 1984), p. 156.

[7]*The Terrors of Ice and Darkness*, trans. John E. Woods (New York: Grove Weidenfeld, 1991), pp. 47, 128; *Die Schrecken des Eises und der Finsternis* (1984; Vienna: Christian Brandstätter; Frankfurt: Fischer, 1987), pp. 61, 151. Further references will be given in the text.

merely invent formulas, "he also pushed thinking mankind forward, raising its estimation of itself in its own eyes and showing it what human reason is capable of." Newton demonstrated that the laws of nature were accessible to human intelligence. In going to the Arctic, Weyprecht hopes to emulate Newton's example, for it is in the barren wasteland that nature's laws are most clearly revealed. Unlike the tropics, where nature appears "in her fullest splendor and lushness, flaunting her Sunday clothes," at the poles she is "naked." Undistracted by details, the eye is drawn to "the overwhelming whole"; attention is focused on "nature's powers" (*Terrors* 85-86; *Schrecken* 103). Weyprecht's approach to research, with its emphasis on observation and the accumulation of data, bears some similarity to the positivistic science condemned by the narrator of *Strahlender Untergang*. Although he seems to regard the relationship between subject and object as neutral and unproblematic, his description of nature as a naked woman betrays the same cognitive interest in subjugation and mastery that characterized the "old" science in the earlier work: through scientific observation, nature's secrets are revealed to the penetrating male gaze.

The ultimate futility of this search for empirical knowledge is underscored by the novel's three historical "Digressions," which recount numerous fruitless attempts to reach the Orient by way of the Arctic. One of the earliest examples from this "chronicle of failure" (*Terrors* 71; *Schrecken* 88) was that of Sir Hugh Willoughby, whose expedition became paradigmatic for those that followed him: "Willoughby's northeast exhibition is the start of a dance of death that will continue into the time of Payer and Weyprecht and beyond" (*Terrors* 46; *Schrecken* 60). When at the end of the nineteenth and the beginning of the twentieth centuries northeast and northwest passages were finally discovered, they remained unnavigable and "of no importance or value to commerce" (*Terrors* 72; *Schrecken* 89). All of which prompts the narrator to ask: "But who would dare claim that the torments and sufferings endured in the search for a passage were pointless? Voyages to hell for routes of no value?" (*Terrors* 72; *Schrecken* 89). The answer to the first question is, of course, the narrator himself, who cannot disguise his view of such expeditions as folly even as he halfheartedly tries to find some meaning in them by pointing out that they did, after all, serve the cause of science, if not trade, by destroying the myths of open polar seas and of paradises in the ice. But the value of such knowledge is clearly disproportional to the suffering expended to achieve it. This is also true of the Austrians' discovery and exploration of the Kaiser Franz Josefs-Land.[8] Obsessed with claiming new lands for Austria and with reaching an ever higher latitude, Payer quickly forgets his scientific principles. "They measure and baptize and suffer" (*Terrors* 177; *Schrecken* 207), the narrator reports. But his christening of the land with names such as Wiener Neustadt Island, Cape Grillparzer, and Crown Prince Rudolf Land

---

[8]The "discovery" was actually the result of a fortuitous accident: the block of ice in which their ship was trapped merely drifted into it.

cannot prevent the desolate and inaccessible piece of real estate from being quickly forgotten. It remains "a forbidden land" (*Terrors* 226; *Schrecken* 262).[9]

If the Austrian expedition was an exercise in futility, Josef Mazzini's voyage is an example of frivolousness. Like his Austrian predecessors, he too is searching for knowledge, but where Weyprecht extolled empirical observation as the path to truth, Mazzini begins with the creations of his own mind. A would-be writer, he attempts to understand the world by testing it against new and imaginative interpretations. He prizes the Arctic as the locale for his stories because an "invented drama" set "in an empty world" was "ultimately much more probable and conceivable than some tropic adventure" (*Terrors* 12; *Schrecken* 22). But Mazzini is not satisfied with mere flights of fancy. He is obsessed with the idea that his inventions also be true; they ought to correspond to reality in the same way that Newton's formulas corresponded for Weyprecht to the laws of nature. Mazzini saw in Payer's memoirs a possible "proof" for one of his invented stories (*Terrors* 13; *Schrecken* 23), and his trip to the Arctic is an attempt to establish the "truth" of his invention. Mazzini's expedition is a parody of the Austrian voyage. The two undertakings are united not only by their ultimate futility — Mazzini disappears in a snowstorm in Spitzbergen — but also by the complexity of the motives that compelled the explorers to subject themselves to such trials in order to achieve goals that were in the end so patently insignificant and inconsequential.

The task of making sense of this falls to the first-person narrator, whose attempt to do so, particularly regarding Mazzini, constitutes the novel's third quest for knowledge. The narrator is determined to find an "explanation" for Mazzini's behavior (*Terrors* 14; *Schrecken* 24), but he is unable to assert his autonomy over the conflicting facts before him. He becomes so preoccupied with Mazzini that he begins to identify with him and to follow him compulsively, as if he, the narrator, were "some piece in a board game" (*Terrors* 15; *Schrecken* 25). By the end of the novel, he is so overwhelmed by his material that he must constantly re-adjust his position vis-a-vis the evidence, describing himself as "a piece of furniture."[10] The narrator's characterization of himself as a helpless object underscores his cognitive impotence. Despite his efforts to maintain the posture of a distanced and objective observer, he cannot avoid regarding his conclusions as subjective and arbitrary:

[9]The folly of such undertakings is also evident in the narrator's description of the quests for the North Pole, an imaginary mathematical point, the "conquest" of which had little scientific significance. As the narrator's account of the Peary/Cook rivalry makes clear, it became "a vanishing point of the vanities" (*Terrors* 144; *Schrecken* 169).

[10]The translation distorts the sense of the original by having the narrator sit in the chair rather than equate himself with it: "I find ways to interpret the facts of Josef Mazzini's disappearance, facts about the ice, find ever new and different ways, and I shift around in them as if in a chair, until every version feels comfortable" (*Terrors* 225). The original has: "Allmählich beginne ich mich einzurichten in der Fülle und Banalität meines Materials, deute mir die Fakten über das Verschwinden Josef Mazzinis, meine Fakten über das Eis, immer anders und neu *und rückte mich in den Versionen zurecht wie ein Möbelstück*" (*Schrecken* 261; my italics).

"And so I arrange the few hints at my disposal, fill the lacunae with guesses, and arriving at the end of a chain of clues, feel how arbitrary it is to say: This is how it was" (*Terrors* 48; *Schrecken* 62). Observation and the accumulation of data do not lead to objective knowledge and truth. In the narrator's words: "Reality is divisible" (*Terrors* 30; *Schrecken* 41).

The narrator's experience is a retraction of the epistemology advocated by Weyprecht. If Newton's discovery of the laws governing the movement of the heavenly bodies demonstrated "what human reason is capable of," as Weyprecht maintained, then the narrator's investigation demonstrates the contrary: the inadequacy of reason to ascertain, order, and interpret the facts. There remains only subjective knowledge: "Each man reported from his own world of ice" (*Terrors* 30; *Schrecken* 41), he observers when reviewing the various reports from the Austrian expedition. Unable to derive any meaningful knowledge from the evidence before him, the narrator regards his task as a failure. He remains, as he says on the last page of the novel, "a chronicler who lacks the comfort of an ending" (*Terrors* 226; *Schrecken* 263).

The futility of this quest for objective knowledge is graphically depicted by Mazzini's encounter with the sled dogs in Spitzbergen. Mazzini learns that the dogs will pull the sled only if the driver succeeds in creating the "illusion" that they are progressing forwards in a straight line. Sled dogs, he discovers, never turn around (*Terrors* 197-98; *Schrecken* 232). This lesson is a metaphor for the facile belief in human progress represented by Weyprecht and problematized by the experiences of the Austrian expedition. The accumulation of empirical knowledge gives the illusion of progress, but such knowledge does not provide insights into what is here regarded as essential: an understanding of human motivation. The narrator is unable to resolve the incongruity between knowledge and suffering in the Austrian expedition; nor can he offer any explanation for Mazzini's obsessive commitment to his frivolous undertaking. Although technology has created the illusion that the world has gotten smaller, the distances have not changed, and, as the narrator reminds the reader in the novel's preface, human beings have remained "pedestrians and runners" (*Terrors* 1; *Schrecken* 9). The novel, which devotes most of its pages to a detailed account of an historical quest for empirical knowledge, leaves the reader instead with unsolved mysteries that neither empirical science nor any rational mode of inquiry can explain.

The narrator directs the reader's attention instead to a deeper level of meaning represented in the references to the myth of Sisyphus and especially to the Biblical story of Job. Weyprecht reads to his crew from the Book of Job, and the longest chapter in the novel, the one in which Payer explores the Franz Josefs-Land, bears the title: "Sketches from the Land of Uz." A lengthy excerpt from the same book of the Bible precedes the chapter chronicling the historical attempts to reach the North Pole. The central passage of that Biblical text summarizes Ransmayr's main theme:

> Man puts his hand to the flinty rock and overturns mountains by the roots. He cuts
> channels in the rocks, and his eye sees every precious thing. He binds up the

streams so that they do not trickle, and the thing that is hid he brings forth to light. But where shall wisdom be found? And where is the place of understanding? (*Terrors* 153; *Schrecken* 178).

Empirical knowledge, which has enabled human beings to exert their mastery over the external world and bring hidden treasures to light, has not brought wisdom; it has not *visualized the sacred* by producing existential insights into the deeper meaning and purpose of life.[11] Like the story of Job, the expeditions to the Arctic depict a fundamental truth; they document not only the inevitability of human suffering but also the ultimate folly of all human endeavors. Wisdom, the novel suggests, results from insight into this inalienable existential fact.

In *The Terrors of Ice and Darkness*, Ransmayr follows the same procedure he employed in *Strahlender Untergang*. In both cases, a quest for empirical knowledge is transformed into a quest for existential meanings. Like the desert in the earlier work, the Arctic forms the backdrop not only for a confrontation with the forces of nature but also for the discovery of a deeper truth. But now the question as to the meaning of science posed in *Strahlender Untergang* is expanded to include the meaning of all rational inquiry. The answer Ransmayr gives, however, is the same: rationality, like science, is meaningless because it provides no answer to Tolstoy's fundamental question: "What shall we do and how shall we live?" By focusing on the question of ultimate meanings, the novel directs attention to a more fundamental level of inquiry, the level of the sacred, where Tolstoy's question can be reasonably posed, if not answered.

In his second novel, *The Last World* [*Die letzte Welt*] (1988), Ransmayr once again blends fact with fiction. In the year 8 A.D. Ovid, also known as Naso because of his prominent nose, was banned by the Roman Emperor Augustus to "the end of the world," to Tomi, a town on the Black Sea (now in Romania). The reasons for the banishment have remained unclear. In Ransmayr's reconstruction, Naso becomes a political *cause célèbre*: he is banished because he represents a threat to the power of Rome. Even the title of his forthcoming *Metamorphoses* is considered an affront to a state "where every edifice was a monument to authority,

---

[11]Peter Sloterdijk has made a similar observation regarding the differences between (technical) knowledge and wisdom:

Wisdom is not dependent on the level of the technical mastery of the world; conversely, the latter presupposes the former when the process of science and technology moves toward an insane state of affairs — as we are observing to-day....However, in the modern type of knowledge, that awareness of life dries up from which the old teachings of wisdom take their inspiration, in order to speak of life and death, love and hate, antagonism and unity, individuality and cosmos, manliness and womanliness. One of the most important motifs in the literature of wisdom is a warning against false cleverness, against 'head' knowledge and learned-ness, against thinking in terms of power and arrogant intellectuality.

Critique of Cynical Reason, trans. Michael Eldred, Theory and Literature 40 (Minneapolis: University of Minnesota Press, 1987), pp. 87-88; *Kritik der zynischen Vernunft*, 2 vols. (Frankfurt: Suhrkamp, 1983), 1: 179.

invoking the stability, the permanence, and immutability of power."[12] It is also suspected that the book might be a *roman à clef*, in which the secrets of prominent Roman citizens would be exposed. Naso seals his political fate when he is invited to speak at the dedication of a new stadium. Forgetting, or deliberately omitting, the requisite litany of homage to the emperor, the senators, and the generals, he opens his address with the words "Citizens of Rome." And instead of extolling the glories of the Roman Empire, he tells the story of the island of Aegina, whose inhabitants were killed by a plague and replaced by a colony of ants. Indignant, the bureaucracy brings the offense to the attention of the emperor, who responds with an indifferent wave of his hand, which is interpreted as meaning: "*Begone. Out of my sight.* Out of the sight of the emperor, however, meant to the end of the world. And the end of the world was Tomi" (*World* 55; *Welt* 73). Before leaving Rome, the historical Ovid burned a copy of his *Metamorphoses*, but the manuscript had already been published. In Ransmayr's novel, Naso burns the original. Cotta, one of his most enthusiastic admirers, travels to Tomi in search of Ovid and the lost masterpiece.

Ransmayr's Rome is a modern bureaucratic state — modeled, he claims, on the former socialist states of Eastern Europe — that has obliterated all vestiges of the sacred and whose public meanings are regarded as alien and unauthentic.[13] It is a state that has "rationalized" every aspect of its citizens' lives, prompting many of them to flee "the boredom of a citizenship whose every ludicrous duty was prescribed" (*World* 93; *Welt* 125). In the name of reason, Rome has stifled every expression of spontaneity, emotion, or instinctual life; it has emptied the reservoir of the sacred whose powers could be sublimated into new public meanings. The "domestification" of these forces is symbolized by the emperor's rhinoceros, a prehistoric beast confined to an inner courtyard and reduced to defending itself against a merciless onslaught of flies and gnats. The emperor's fascination with his pet suggests an unconscious attraction to the primitive vitality he has so successfully obliterated throughout his empire but which continues to survive in Naso's elegies, stories, and dramas. By focusing on these instinctual forces, which were once part of Rome's past, Naso commits the unspeakable crime: he proclaims the return of the repressed. "And had it not been Naso, with his elegies, his tales and dramas, who had stirred forgotten memories and reminded Rome, now a pallid body politic, of its archaic and wild passions?" (*World* 70-71; *Welt* 93), Cotta asks. The triumph of reason has created an efficient state, but in suppressing "archaic and wild passions" it also has suppressed love, compassion, and empathy, the forces of Eros, whom Freud described as one of the parents of human

[12]Ransmayr, *The Last World: A Novel with an Ovidian Repertory*, trans. John E. Woods (New York: Grove Weidenfeld, 1990), p. 33; *Die letzte Welt. Mit einem Ovidischen Repertoire* (Nördlingen: Franz Greno, 1988), p. 44. Future references will be given in the text.

[13]"In Eastern Europe, like Augustan Rome, they were trying to make people believe that power could be eternal." Quoted (in English) by Cohen.

civilization.[14] Naso's story of the end of the world, told to Cotta by Echo, describes the final consequence of the repression of these forces. It is a vision of a desacralized world populated by a race of human beings of stone,

> a brood of mineral-like hardness, with hearts of basalt, eyes of jade, without feelings, without a language of love, but likewise without any stirrings of hate, sympathy, or grief, as implacable, as deaf and durable as the rocks of this coast (*World* 126-127; *Welt* 169-70).

The archaic passions that Rome has suppressed are still present in Tomi, where, Cotta discovers, the forgotten Roman past is "still wild and alive" (*World* 71; *Welt* 94). An idle young aristocrat who has led a life of "ease and security" and a member of that "elegant little audience" that constitutes Naso's staunchest supporters, Cotta journeys to Tomi in order to find "the truth about the poet" (*World* 34, 110, 111; *Welt* 45, 147, 148). His journey precipitates a confrontation between the unauthentic public meanings of civilized Rome and the deeper truth of Ovid's mythical world, whose motto is: "Nothing retains its form" (*World* 9; *Welt* 15). These words, scribbled on a piece of cloth by Naso's servant Pythagoras and discovered by Cotta, characterize a town inhabited by human beings who transform themselves into wolves, into stone, or into birds. In Tomi, Ovid's *Metamorphoses* have become reality. For Cotta, the inexplicable petrification of Battus is a mockery of Roman reason, reducing it to nothing more than "a collection of empty sentences and phrases" (*World* 167; *Welt* 220-21). Cotta seeks Naso because he believes he is the only one who could explain these "riddles" and lead him back to the "compact clarity of Roman reason" (*World* 169; *Welt* 223). But what began as a search for a lost poet and his manuscript becomes much more. As in *The Terrors of Ice and Darkness*, the quest for empirical knowledge leads instead to a confrontation with the sacred, with the realm in which fundamental existential meanings are generated.

The sacred is closely associated with what anthropologist Victor Turner has called "anti-structure," which he defines as the "dissolution of normative social structure, with its role-sets, statuses, jural rights and duties, and so on."[15] Anti-structure, Turner insists, is not merely "a structural reversal, a mirror-imaging of 'profane' workaday socioeconomic structure." It implies "the liberation of human capacities of cognition, affect, volition, creativity, etc., from the normative constraints incumbent upon occupying a sequence of social statuses..." It is a moment

---

[14]Sigmund Freud, *Civilization and Its Discontents*, trans. James Strachey (New York: Norton, 1961), p. 53. The other parent is Necessity. Significantly, Rome is also described as "the realm of necessity and reason" (*World* 219; *Welt* 287).

[15]Victor Turner, "Liminal to Liminoid, in Play, Flow, and Ritual: An Essay in Comparative Symbology," *Rice University Studies* 60.3 (1974): 60.

of "pure potentiality"; it contains "the germ of future social developments, of societal change."[16]

Tomi, which is characterized by its physical as well as its spiritual distance from Rome, resembles this anti-structural space. It is governed by its own logic and its own sense of time. Even the order of nature is overturned. Two years of winter are followed by a spring that brings with it plants never before seen in Tomi and by a summer with spiders as large as a fist. In the courtyard of Naso's house in Trachila, a mulberry tree stands "soft and green" among patches of snow and frozen puddles (*World* 9; *Welt* 15), and in his garden giant sub-tropical ferns emerge from the snow-covered earth. Surrounded by an impenetrable wall of plants and strewn with ancient stones, granite tablets, columns, and menhirs, the garden recalls "a ravaged sculpture garden or a cemetery." Thousands of slugs, "creeping in layers, in tangles," cover the stones. Primitive symbols of both sexuality and death, they emit an eerie "song of pain" when Pythagoras pours vinegar on them to remove them from the headstones, and Cotta sees "how the motion of death entered into the tough, moist webwork of feelers and bodies — hasty, twitching life" (*World* 36-37; *Welt* 48-49). Overflowing with primal symbols of life and death, this garden, which Cotta visits twice in the novel, recalls those "asocial powers of life and death" that Turner associates with anti-structure and that are also at the vortex of the sacred.[17]

Cotta's encounter with these elemental forces takes the form of a rite of passage. According to Turner, who has investigated these transformations in pre-industrial societies, the first phase of such a rite is marked by a separation that "clearly demarcates sacred space and time from profane or secular space and time." It is followed by an anti-structural, liminal phase, which may be apprehended as sacred, during which the subject is "temporarily undefined, beyond the normative social structure." During the liminal phase, the subjects undergo a leveling process, "in which signs of their preliminal status are destroyed and signs of their liminal non-status are applied." Their symbolic "death" is followed by the third phase, their rebirth as new members of society.[18]

Cotta's departure from the normative, structured society of Rome is the first stage of this process. Like the initiates in a rite of passage, he abandons his old identity and embarks on a quest for new meanings and a new self as he passes through the anti-structural world of Tomi. This liminal phase is articulated most clearly during Cotta's second visit to Trachila. Marked by the ambivalence typical of liminality, Cotta "hovered between the imperial, indisputable reality of Rome

[16]Turner, pp. 75-76.

[17]Turner, p. 59.

[18]Turner, pp. 56-59. Turner borrows the tripartite structure of rites of passage from Arnold van Gennep, *The Rites of Passage*, trans. Monika B. Vizedom and Gabrielle L. Caffee (London: Routledge and Keegan Paul, 1909). See also Turner, *The Ritual Process: Structure and Anti-Structure* (1969; Ithaca: Cornell University Press, 1977), esp. chapter 3.

and the incomprehensible mysteries of the town of iron" (*World* 175; *Welt* 231). The normal notions of time disintegrate: "Time slowed now, stood still, fell back into the past"; and: "Times and seasons laid their names aside, intermingled, fused" (*World* 181, 184; *Welt* 238, 241). His identity is progressively "leveled" as he is described as "a wanderer, a reptile, an insect" (*World* 172; *Welt* 226) and finally as "a larva embedded in sand, moss, and linden-green lichens, waiting to awaken" (*World* 176; *Welt* 232). Before this awakening, however, Cotta must "die" and be reborn. This "death" is symbolized in his arduous journey to Trachila. He must pass through a labyrinth of valleys and ravines; his night alone in the mountains is described as an "ordeal" ["Prüfung"] (*World* 175; *Welt* 231). Accompanied by circling vultures as he travels through the mountains, he recalls the story of two shepherds buried by an avalanche, their eyes and faces, their very identities, eaten away by the scavenging birds. Similarly, Cotta's ordeal results in the "death" of his old identity and the birth of a new one. Like the larva transformed into a new creature, he leaves his old self behind, observing it from a distance: "He heard his voice far in the distance, he was outside himself now, somewhere high up in the shimmering rocks, watching a madman crouched in the ruins of Trachila..." (*World* 183; *Welt* 241).

Cotta emerges from this liminal experience with a new understanding of the world and of himself. For the first time, "the tormenting conflict between Rome's reason and the Black Sea's incomprehensible realities dissolved" (*World* 184; *Welt* 241). The mysteries of Tomi are now "riddles no longer" (*World* 218; *Welt* 285). Naso's world, which receives its apotheosis at the end of the novel in Cotta's vision of Mount Olympus, comes to symbolize a deeper truth. It conveys an unmediated knowledge that goes beyond the "empty sentences and phrases" of Roman rationality and that renders superfluous any attempt at rational description: "Reality, once discovered, no longer needed recording."[19] Convinced that he has acquired a new identity as a member of this world, Cotta returns to the mountains at the end of the novel to look for his own name on one of Pythagoras's semaphores.

But this new identity is an ambivalent one. Cotta remains uncertain of his own sanity and is regarded by the inhabitants of Tomi as mad. And when, on the last page of the book, he calls his name into the mountains, the returning echo, described as "broken and familiar" ["so gebrochen und so vertraut"] (*World* 219; *Welt* 288), offers an ambiguous comment on the new identity he believes he has acquired.

In terms of the tripartite rite of passage, Cotta's identity is necessarily obscure because it is not anchored in any identifiable social reality. He has remained in the realm of anti-structure; the third stage of the rite, the re-integration into society, is missing. Cotta's encounter with the mysteries of Tomi has not led to a new social identity. It coincides instead with a withdrawal into himself. When he visited

---

[19]"Die Erfindung der Wirklichkeit bedurfte keiner Aufzeichnungen mehr" (*World* 219; *Welt* 287).

Trachila for the first time, he thought that the only appropriate form of existence there was "this total retreat into himself" ["dieses völlige Zurücksinken in sich selbst"] (*World* 32; *Welt* 42). In an interview, Ransmayr used these same words to describe what he would regard as a "paradise." "I *seek* that, almost as a utopia," he said, adding: "What is so terrible about an overgrown, blooming wilderness without us?"[20] A total retreat into oneself may be one response to a desacralized world, but, as we have seen in Thomas Bernhard, it is not one that human beings can maintain for long. As Peter Berger and Thomas Luckmann have stressed: "Human being is impossible in a closed sphere of quiescent interiority. Human being must ongoingly externalize itself in activity."[21] *The Last World* demonstrates the impossibility of either alternative. Cotta has established a relationship to a deeper reality, but in a society that is "opaque to the sacred" this deeper reality cannot be employed to create new, authentic public meanings. The sacred can be experienced only by withdrawing from the social world and its communicative web. Like the experimental subject in *Strahlender Untergang*, Cotta can only say "I" at the margins of society. In this respect, Ransmayr's work, like Gerhard Roth's and Peter Sloterdijk's, reflects the *destruction of the public sphere* and the resultant *privatization of meaning*. For Roth, this meant withdrawal into a personal world of fantasy or madness; for Sloterdijk, it meant the search a new mode of Being; and for Ransmayr, it means escape to the margins: to the desert, to the Arctic, or to the end of the world.

The Last World has been well received by both critics and the general public.[22] Given the novel's esoteric subject matter, its wide popularity is surprising. Ransmayr's considerable talent as a writer and the beauty of his prose are at least partly responsible for the novel's positive reception, but a more convincing explanation must be sought on the level of content. *The Last World* addresses two aspects of what might be termed a postmodern sensibility: a critique of modernity

---

[20]"Ich *suche* das, geradezu als Utopie....Was aber ist so schrecklich an einer wuchernden, blühenden Wildnis ohne uns?" Interview with Renate Just, "Erfolg macht müde," *Zeitmagazin* 16 Dec. 1988: 50. Cf. also *The Terrors of Ice and Darkness*: As the First World War is breaking out, the narrator attributes the following thoughts to Julius Payer, the discoverer of the Franz Josefs-Land: "I say: The silent man now realizes that he really did discover a paradise" (*Terrors* 224; *Schrecken* 260).

[21]Peter L. Berger and Thomas Luckmann, *The Social Construction of Reality: A Treatise in the Sociology of Knowledge* (New York: Doubleday, 1966), p. 52.

[22]See for example Harald Wieser, "Eine Flaschenpost aus der Antike," *Der Spiegel* 42 (12 Sept. 1988): 226-37; Frank Schirrmacher, "Bücher aus Asche, Leiber aus Ameisen. Endlich ein neues Talent: Christoph Ransmayr und sein sprachgewaltiger Einbildungsroman *Die letzte Welt*," *Frankfurter Allgemeine Zeitung* 17 Sept. 1988, Beilage: 5; and Volker Hage, "Mein Name sei Ovid. Ein großer Roman: Christoph Ransmayrs *Die letzte Welt*," *Die Zeit* 7 Oct. 1988, Beilage: 1-2. As of spring 1990, over 200,000 copies had been sold in German; translations into twenty languages were being planned.

and an evocation of those deeper meanings that modernity has allegedly destroyed.[23] In a technological society, Ransmayr's novel depicts a poeticized world and reminds the reader of the existence of a deeper reality. In so doing, it assumes a function that has traditionally been performed by religion: the mediation of the sacred. As a critique of modernity, Ransmayr's work echoes Daniel Bell's contention that only a return to religion can heal the malaise of modern society.[24] But this can only happen if the sacred, a sense of deeper, collectively shared meanings, is integrated once again into the public sphere, a prospect for which Ransmayr does not seem to hold out much hope.

[23] Cf. Kurt Bartsch, who attributes the book's success to its affinities with the postmodern *Zeitgeist*, specifically with "the preference for past epochs, the apocalyptic conjuration of the end of time, and with connoisseurship." "Dialog mit Antike und Mythos. Christoph Ransmayrs Ovid-Roman *Die letzte Welt*," *Modern Austrian Literature* 23.34 (1990): 130.

[24] Bell:

My concern with religion goes back to what I assume is the constitutive character of culture: the wheel of questions that brings one back to the existential predicaments, the awareness in men of their finiteness and the inexorable limits to their power...and the consequent effort to find a coherent answer to reconcile them to the human condition. Since that awareness touches the deepest springs of consciousness, I believe that a culture which has become aware of the limits in exploring the mundane will turn, at some point, to the effort to recover the sacred.

"Modernism and Capitalism," *Partisan Review* 45 (1978): 221. See also Bell's *The Cultural Contradictions of Capitalism* (New York: Basic Books, 1976).

Conclusion

IN HIS ESSAY "THE END OF PHILOSOPHY and the Task of Thinking," Heidegger claimed that science has become so dominant in the modern world that it has become identical with philosophy:

> Philosophy is ending in the present age. It has found its place in the scientific attitude of socially active humanity. But the mental characteristic of this scientific attitude is its cybernetic, that is, technological character. The need to ask about modern technology is presumably dying out to the same extent that technology more definitely characterizes and regulates the appearance of the totality of the world and the position of man in it.[1]

Heidegger's is but one voice in a chorus of criticism directed against scientific rationality. This chorus has included, among others, Nietzsche, Max Weber, members of the Frankfurt School, and, more recently, several of the thinkers discussed in the introduction to this book. These scholarly disputes have found an echo on a societal level in the current debates on medical ethics, genetic engineering, nuclear energy and armaments, and the environment, all of which question the intrusion of science into the lifeworld and its interference in areas that had been traditionally regarded as sacred.[2]

At issue are fundamental epistemological and ethical questions: Ought science still to be regarded as a privileged mode of inquiry whose discoveries, pronouncements, and products must be accepted unconditionally? Is there but one rationality, namely scientific rationality? Does science provide the only model for reacting with the world? These questions all attempt to "reconstruct" knowledge, as Raskin and Bernstein called their re-evaluation and re-examination of the role of science

---

[1]Martin Heidegger, "The End of Philosophy and the Task of Thinking," in *Basic Writings*, ed. David Farrell Krell (New York: Harper and Row, 1977), p. 376.

[2]Cf. also Jürgen Habermas, "New Social Movements," *Telos* 49 (fall 1981): 33-37. These debates have, of course, not always gone forward in accordance with the principle of reasoned argumentation. Witness, for example, the recent disruptions of university lectures and conferences on medical ethics in Germany and Austria by activists who sought to prevent even the *discussion* of euthanasia or genetic engineering. See Peter Singer, "On Being Silenced in Germany," *New York Review of Books* 15 August 1991: 36-42.

and rationality in society.[3] This reconstruction is implied in Friedrich Dürren-matt's attempts to "save" rationality and science by adopting Popper's critical rationalism as well as in the critical portrayal of scientific rationality in works by Thomas Bernhard, Gerhard Roth, Peter Sloterdijk, and Christoph Ransmayr.

At the heart of these questions is an attempt to confront the traditional dualism of facts and values, the notion that science, as a neutral mode of inquiry, deals with "objective" facts that are distinct from "subjective" values. As Wayne Booth has pointed out, this distinction has become a widely accepted tenet of modernity:

> If the word dogma is applicable to any general notion that cannot, for the believer, be brought into question, the belief that you cannot and indeed should not allow your values to intrude upon your cognitive life — that thought and knowledge and fact are on one side and affirmations of value on the other — has been until recently a dogma for all right-thinking moderns.[4]

The dualism of facts and values continues to reverberate in Dürrenmatt's assertion that science is "value-free" and "beyond good and evil" as well as in Hochhuth's attempt to justify his own historiography and dramaturgy by references to science. The other writers, by contrast, seem convinced of the self-referentiality of rational methods and of the inevitable entwinement of the objective and the subjective. Thomas Bernhard's dismantling of the subject/object dichotomy, for example, reveals "objective" knowledge as a projection of "subjective" values and desires. Similarly, the equation of rationality with instrumentality and of science with domination in works by Roth, Sloterdijk, and Ransmayr suggests that rationality and science are not neutral but are in fact invested with interests.

The vision of science and scientific rationality presented by the last four writers is very often a minimalist one. Some of the recurring ideas in their works — that scientific rationality is purely instrumental, that science has substituted knowledge of facts for real wisdom, or that it has destroyed deeper meanings — betray a tendency to equate science with a narrowly conceived positivism, one which, as Edward Davenport has pointed out, has perhaps never existed:

> Like all devils, positivism has become a blank screen onto which are projected the anxieties and hidden desires of literary critics, philosophers, and social theorists. We wish to escape the threats (dystopic social control, nuclear annihilation, or

---

[3]Marcus G. Raskin and Herbert J. Bernstein, *New Ways of Knowing: The Sciences, Society, and Reconstructive Knowledge* (Totowa, New Jersey: Rowman and Littlefield, 1987). As Habermas has observed, such debates are often initiated by marginal groups, which have assumed the discursive function formerly exercised by the public sphere. See the discussion in the introduction.

[4]Wayne Booth, *Modern Dogma and the Rhetoric of Assent*, University of Notre Dame Ward-Phillips Lectures in English Language and Literature 5 (Notre Dame: Notre Dame University Press; Chicago: University of Chicago Press, 1974), p. 13.

simply the deadening of emotional and aesthetic response) that are all too easy to blame on the growth of scientific knowledge.[5]

As Popper (and Dürrenmatt) have shown, science also implies criticism, discourse, and an outspoken humility about claims to knowledge and assertions of truth. To be sure, instrumental reason, manipulation, and control are all aspects of modernity, but the simple equation of reason with manipulation and of science with domination is reductionist. As Neil Wilson has observed: "A totalitarian world characterized by the complete subjection of every action, emotion, thought or decision to an instrumental rationality simply does not exist."[6]

This preoccupation with scientific rationality reflects a concern for epistemological questions that is a hallmark of literary modernism. In the works of Bernhard, Roth, Sloterdijk, and Ransmayr, however, there is also evidence of a postmodern turn to ontology, which, according to Brian McHale, is as characteristic of postmodernist fiction as epistemology was of modernist works. Epistemology and ontology are, of course, interconnected. "Intractable epistemological uncertainty," McHale writes, "becomes at a certain point ontological plurality or instability: push epistemological questions far enough and they 'tip over' into ontological questions." Postmodernist texts, McHale maintains, typically pose questions such as: "What is the world?; What kinds of worlds are there, how are they constituted, and how do they differ?; What happens when different kinds of worlds are placed in confrontation, or when boundaries between worlds are violated?" These texts exhibit what McHale, borrowing a term from Foucault, calls "heterotopia," the juxtaposition of several incommensurable and discontinuous worlds.[7] A plurality of co-existent worlds is suggested in the autonomous subjective universes of Bernhard's protagonists as well as in the schizophrenic existences (another hallmark of

---

[5]He continues two paragraphs later: "The demonization of positivism has led to historical ignorance of the positivist legacy and to hostility toward science, rationality, and critical debate, insofar as these are associated with the discredited philosophy." Edward Davenport, "The Devils of Positivism," in *Literature and Science: Theory and Practice*, ed. Stuart Peter-freund (Boston: Northeastern University Press, 1990), pp. 26-27. That positivism has become something of a straw man was already evident in the German positivist dispute of the 1960s, none of whose participants, least of all Karl Popper, who was so accused, admitted to being a positivist. See *The Positivist Dispute in German Sociology*, trans. Glyn Adey and David Frisby (London: Heinemann, 1976).

[6]Neil Wilson, "Punching Out the Enlightenment: A Discussion of Peter Sloterdijk's *Kritik der zynischen Vernunft*," *New German Critique* 41 (1987): 66.

[7]Brian McHale, *Postmodernist Fiction* (New York: Methuen, 1987), pp. 10, 11, 44. Similarly, Stuart Parkes, writing on the German novel in the 1980s, observes: "Multi-dimensionality is literally the order of the day." "Introduction," *Literature on the Theshold: The German Novel in the 1980s*, eds. Arthur Williams, Stuart Parkes, and Roland Smith (Oxford: Berg, 1990), p. 5. See also Foucault, *The Order of Things: An Archaeology of the Human Sciences* (1966; New York: Random House, 1970), p. xviii, and David Harvey, *The Condition of Postmodernity: An Inquiry into the Origins of Cultural Change* (London: Basil Blackwell, 1989), esp. pp. 39-65.

postmodernism)[8] of some of Roth's figures. It is also suggested by the Mesmerists' and van Leyden's attempts to articulate a new mode of Being in Sloterdijk's *Der Zauberbaum* as well as by the juxtaposition of Tomi and Rome, the realms of the sacred and the profane, in Ransmayr's *The Last World*.

The turn to ontology results from the postmodernist suspicion of all totalizing metanarratives that lay claim to a privileged interpretation of reality.[9] But are these works a manifestation of "a postmodernism of resistance" or of "a postmodernism of reaction"?[10] By depicting alternative worlds and oppositional modes of thought, they do imply a critique of the status quo and thus contribute to "resistance." But they also exhibit a nostalgia for an idealized, *pre*modern mode of existence. Gerhard Roth's search for a purified, mystical language, Sloterdijk's desire to overcome the division of subject and object (which also preoccupied Bernhard), and Ransmayr's attempt to recover a sense of the sacred all betray a desire for a lost transparency, synthesis, and wholeness, which, they imply, modernity has destroyed.[11]

This critique of modernity is a reaction to a technological society that presents scientific rationality as the only source of meanings. For Bernhard, Roth, Sloterdijk, and Ransmayr, the public sphere, as a locus of discourse free of domination, has disintegrated. Meanings, if they are to be found at all, can, they suggest, be discovered only subjectively. In their works, human beings seem to exist in isolation; their search for meaning and identity must be undertaken alone. The critique of science spills over into a critique of rationality *tout court*; communication and discourse are as suspect as positivist science.

Poised at the frontier of the modern and the postmodern, these works question one of modernity's most cherished ideals: the possibility of discursively articulating and consensually maintaining collectively shared, authentic public meanings. As Peter Berger has reminded us, an authentic identity and authentic public meanings are irrevocably linked to the view of men and women as members of a community: "Identity, with its appropriate attachments of psychological reality,

---

[8]See Frederick Jameson, "Postmodernism and Consumer Society," in *The Anti-Aesthetic: Essays on Postmodern Culture,* ed. Hal Foster (Seattle: Bay Press, 1983), pp. 111-25.

[9]It is in this sense that Jean-François Lyotard describes the postmodern as "incredulity toward metanarratives." *The Postmodern Condition: A Report on Knowledge*, trans. Geoff Bennington and Brian Massumi, Theory and History of Literature 10 (1979; Minneapolis: University of Minnesota Press, 1984), p. xxiv.

[10]Hal Foster, "Postmodernism: A Preface," in *The Anti-Aesthetic*, p. xii.

[11]Cf. Martin Lüdke's characterization of postmodernism as "the epitome of lost commitment." "German Literature on the Theshold of the Twenty-First Century: A Critic's Perspective," trans. Arthur Williams, in *Literature on the Threshold*, p. 345.

is always identity within a specific, socially constructed world."[12] In works by Bernhard, Roth, Sloterdijk, and Ransmayr, the protagonists' turn away from this world is at once a critique of modernity and a quest for an indeterminate postmodern alternative. In search of this alternative, they embark on a potentially endless *voyage interieur* that leads them further away from the idea of a communicatively supported collective and that risks fatally disentangling them from the web of communicative action in which they, like all human beings, are inextricably implicated.

[12]Peter Berger, "Identity as a Problem in the Sociology of Knowledge," *The Sociology of Knowledge*, eds. James E. Curtis and John W. Petras (New York: Praeger, 1970), p. 378. Italicized in original.

Works Consulted

Primary Sources

Bernhard, Thomas. *Frost*. 1963. Frankfurt: Insel/Suhrkamp, 1972.

——. *Verstörung*. Frankfurt: Insel/Suhrkamp, 1967.

——. *Gargoyles* [*Verstörung*]. Trans. Richard and Clara Winston. New York: Knopf, 1970; Chicago: University of Chicago Press, 1986.

——. *Das Kalkwerk*. Frankfurt: Suhrkamp, 1970.

——. *The Lime Works*. Trans. Sophie Wilkins. New York: Knopf, 1973; Chicago: University of Chicago Press, 1986.

——. *Korrektur*. Frankfurt: Suhrkamp, 1975.

——. *Correction*. Trans. Sophie Wilkins. New York: Knopf, 1979.

——. *Beton*. Frankfurt: Suhrkamp, 1982.

——. *Concrete*. Trans. David McLintock. New York: Knopf, 1984.

——. *Der Untergeher*. Frankfurt: Suhrkamp, 1983.

——. *The Loser*. Trans. Jack Dawson. New York: Knopf, 1991.

——. *Holzfällen: Eine Erregung*. Frankfurt: Suhrkamp, 1984.

——. *Woodcutters*. Trans. David McLintock. New York: Knopf, 1987.

——. *Alte Meister: Komödie*. Frankfurt: Suhrkamp, 1985.

——. *Old Masters: A Comedy*. Trans. Ewald Osers. London: Quartet, 1989.

——. *Auslöschung: Ein Zerfall*. Frankfurt: Suhrkamp, 1986.

Dürrenmatt, Friedrich. *Werkausgabe in dreißig Bänden*. Zürich: Diogenes, 1980.

——. *Romulus the Great*. Trans. Gerhard Nellhaus. *Friedrich Dürrenmatt: Plays and Essays*. Ed. Volker Sander. The German Library 89. 1964. New York: Continuum, 1982.

——. *Achterloo: Eine Komödie in zwei Akten*. Zürich: Diogenes, 1983.

——. *Minotaurus: Eine Ballade*. Zürich: Diogenes, 1985.

——, and Charlotte Kerr. *Rollenspiele: Protokoll einer fiktiven Inszenierung und Achterloo III*. Zürich: Diogenes, 1986.

——. *Der Auftrag oder Vom Beobachten des Beobachters der Beobachter: Novelle in vierundzwanzig Sätzen*. Zürich: Diogenes, 1986.

——. *The Assignment, Or On the Observing of the Observer of the Observers: Novelle in Twenty-Four Sentences*. Trans. Joel Agee. New York: Random House, 1988.

——. *Versuche*. Zürich: Diogenes, 1988.

——. *Durcheinandertal*. Zürich: Diogenes, 1989.

——. "Man stirbt. Und plötzlich blickt man zum Mond. *Zeit*-Gespräch mit Friedrich Dürrenmatt." Interview with Michael Haller. *Die Zeit* 28 Dec. 1990.

——. *Turmbau: Stoffe IV-IX*. Zürich: Diogenes, 1990.

——. *Über die Grenzen* [Interviews]. Zürich: pendo-verlag, 1990.

——. *Kants Hoffnung: Zwei politische Reden. Zwei Gedichte aus dem Nachlaß*. Zürich: Diogenes, 1991.

Hochhuth, Rolf. *Guerillas: Tragödie in 5 Akten*. Reinbek: Rowohlt, 1970.

——. *Die Hebamme: Komödie. Erzählungen. Gedichte. Essays*. Die Bücher der Neunzehn 203. Reinbek: Rowohlt, 1971.

——. *Krieg und Klassenkrieg: Studien*. Reinbek: Rowohlt, 1971.

——. *Räuber-Rede. Drei deutsche Vorwürfe: Schiller/Lessing/Geschwister Scholl*. Reinbek: Rowohlt, 1982.

——. *Judith: Trauerspiel*. Reinbek: Rowohlt, 1984.

Ransmayr, Christoph. *Strahlender Untergang: Ein Entwässerungsprojekt oder die Entdeckung des Wesentlichen*. Vienna: Christian Brandstätter, 1982. Photographs by Willy Puchner.

——. *Die Schrecken des Eises und der Finsternis*. Frankfurt: Fischer, 1987. Vienna: Christian Brandstätter, 1984.

——. *The Terrors of Ice and Darkness*. Trans. John E. Woods. New York: Grove Weidenfeld, 1991.

——. *Die letzte Welt. Mit einem Ovidischen Repertoire*. Nördlingen: Franz Greno, 1988.

——. *The Last World: A Novel with an Ovidian Repertory*. Trans. John E. Woods. New York: Grove Weidenfeld, 1990.

——. "Erfolg macht müde." Interview with Renate Just. *Zeitmagazin* 16 Dec. 1988.

Roth, Gerhard. *die autobiographie des albert einstein: Fünf Kurzromane*. Frankfurt: Fischer, 1972.

——. *Der große Horizont*. Frankfurt: Suhrkamp, 1974.

——. *Ein neuer Morgen*. Frankfurt: Suhrkamp, 1976.

——. "Keine Sehnsucht nach Stillstand. Mit Gerhard Roth sprach Kurt Wimmer." *Kleine Zeitung* (Graz) 5 June 1977.

——. *Winterreise*. Frankfurt: Fischer, 1978.

——. *Der stille Ozean*. Frankfurt: Fischer, 1980.

——. *On the Boarderline* [sic]: *A Documentary Record. Grenzland: Ein dokumentarisches Protokoll*. Vienna: Hannibal, 1981.

——. *Die schönen Bilder beim Trabrennen*. Frankfurt: Fischer, 1982.

——. "Eismeer des Schweigens. Ernst Herbeck: 'Alexander' — Ausgewählte Texte 1961-1981." *Die Zeit* 14 Jan. 1983.

——. *Landläufiger Tod*. Frankfurt: Fischer, 1984.

——. *Am Abgrund*. Frankfurt: Fischer, 1986.

——. "Die Fürchterlichsten sind die Gebildeten." Interview with Ditta Rudle. *Wochenpresse* (Vienna) 17 July 1987: 38-40.

——. "Das allmähliche Verstummen der Sprache." *Die Zeit* 16 Oct. 1987.

——. "Labyrinth der Fälschungen." *Die Zeit* 21 Jan. 1988.

——. *Der Untersuchungsrichter: Die Geschichte eines Entwurfs*. Frankfurt: Fischer, 1988.

——. *Über Bienen. Mit Fotos von Franz Killmeyer*. Vienna: Jugend und Volk, 1989.

Sloterdijk, Peter. *Kritik der zynischen Vernunft*. 2 vols. Frankfurt: Suhrkamp, 1983.

——. *Critique of Cynical Reason*. Trans. Michael Eldred. Theory and History of Literature 40. Minneapolis: University of Minnesota Press, 1987.

——. *Der Zauberbaum: Die Entstehung der Psychoanalyse im Jahr 1785. Ein epischer Versuch zur Philosophie der Psychologie*. Frankfurt: Suhrkamp, 1985.

——. *Kopernikanische Mobilmachung und ptolemäische Abrüstung* Frankfurt: Suhrkamp, 1987.

——. *Eurotaoismus: Zur Kritik der politischen Kinetik*. Frankfurt: Suhrkamp, 1989.

Secondary Sources

Thomas Bernhard

Barthofer, Alfred. "Existenz von der Weltstange. Anmerkungen zu Thomas Bernhards Roman *Korrektur*." *Acta Germanica* 10 (1977): 319-330.

Buchka, Peter. "Nörgelei als Widerstand. Thomas Bernhards neues Prosabuch *Beton*." *Süddeutsche Zeitung* 6 Oct. 1982.

Falcke, Eberhard. "Abschreiben. Eine Ablehnung. Eberhard Falcke über Thomas Bernhards Roman 'Auslöschung. Ein Zerfall.'" *Der Spiegel* 40 (3 Nov 1986): 256-60.

Fetz, Gerald. "Thomas Bernhard and the 'Modern Novel.'" *The Modern German Novel*. Ed. Keith Bullivant. Leamington Spa, UK: Berg, 1987, 89-108.

vom Hofe, Gerhard. "Ecce Lazarus. Autor-Existenz und 'Privat'-Metaphysik in Thomas Bernhards autobiographischen Schriften." *duitse kroniek* 3 (1982): 18-36.

Leser, Norbert. "Warum Bernhard (noch) kein Moralist ist." *profil* (Vienna) 43 (21 Oct. 1985): 74.

Leventhal, Robert S. "The Rhetoric of Anarcho-Nihilistic Murder: Thomas Bernhard's *Das Kalkwerk*." *Modern Austrian Literature* 21.3-4 (1988): 19-38.

Lindenmayr, Heinrich. *Totalität und Beschränkung: Eine Untersuchung zu Thomas Bernhards Roman "Das Kalkwerk*." Hochschulschriften: Literaturwissenschaft 50. Königstein: Forum Academicum, 1982.

Mauch, Gudrun. "Thomas Bernhards Roman *Korrektur*. Die Spannung zwischen dem erzählenden und dem erlebenden Erzähler." *Österreich in Geschichte und Literatur* 4 (1979): 207-19.

Michaelis, Rolf. "Vernichtungsjubel. Thomas Bernhards monumentales Prosawerk *Auslöschung — Ein Zerfall*. Politisches Pamphlet und Roman der Trauer." *Die Zeit* 3 Oct. 1986.

Pail, Gerhard. "Perspektivität in Thomas Bernhards *Holzfällen*." *Modern Austrian Literature* 21.3-4 (1988): 51-68.

Petersen, Jürgen H. "Beschreibung einer sinnentleerten Welt. Erzählthematik und Erzählverfahren in Thomas Bernhards Romanen." *Bernhard: Annäherungen*. Ed. Manfred Jurgensen. Queensland Studies in German Language and Literature 8. Bern: Francke, 1981, 143-176.

Petrasch, Ingrid. *Die Konstitution von Wirklichkeit in der Prosa Thomas Bernhards: Sinnbildlichkeit und groteske Überzeichnung*. Münchener Studien zur literarischen Kultur in Deutschland 2. Frankfurt: Peter Lang, 1987.

Reinhardt, Hartmut. "Das kranke Subjekt. Überlegungen zur monologischen Reduktion bei Thomas Bernhard." *Germanisch-romanische Monatshefte* NS 26 (1976): 334-56.

Roberts, David. "Korrektur der Korrektur? Zu Thomas Bernhards Lebenskunstwerk 'Korrektur.'" *Bernhard: Annäherungen*. Ed. Manfred Jurgensen. Queensland Studies in German Language and Literature 8. Bern: Francke, 1981, 199-214.

Rossbacher, Karlheinz. "Thomas Bernhard: *Das Kalkwerk* (1970)." *Deutsche Romane des 20. Jahrhunderts: Neue Interpretationen*. Ed. Paul Michael Lützeler. Königstein: Athenäum, 1983, 372-87.

Schmidt-Dengler, Wendelin. "Bernhards Attacke auf die ererbte Last der Geschichte." *Kleine Zeitung* (Graz) 27 Feb. 1987.

Seydel, Bernd. *Die Vernunft der Winterkälte: Gleichgültigkeit als Equilibrismus im Werk Thomas Bernhards*. Epistemata. Würzburger Wissenschaftliche Schriften. Reihe Literaturwissenschaft 22. Würzburg: Königshausen und Neumann, 1986.

Sharp, Francis Michael. "Thomas Bernhard: Literary Cryogenics or Art on Ice." *Modern Austrian Literature* 21.3-4 (1988): 201-15.

Sorg, Berhard. *Thomas Bernhard*. Autorenbücher 7. Munich: Beck, 1977.

Weinzierl, Ulrich. "Bernhard als Erzieher: Thomas Bernhards *Auslöschung*." *German Quarterly* 63 (1990): 455-61.

Friedrich Dürrenmatt

Knapp, Mona, and Gerhard P. Knapp. "Recht — Gerechtigkeit — Politik. Zur Genese der Begriffe im Werk Friedrich Dürrenmatts." *Friedrich Dürrenmatt II*. Ed. Heinz Ludwig Arnold. text + kritik 56. Munich: edition text + kritik, 1977, 23-40.

Knapp, Gerhard P. *Friedrich Dürrenmatt*. Sammlung Metzler 196. Stuttgart: Metzler, 1980.

Knopf, Jan. *Friedrich Dürrenmatt*. 3rd ed. Autorenbücher 3. Munich: Beck, 1980.

——. "Sprachmächtigkeiten." *Facetten: Studien zum 60. Geburtstag Friedrich Dürrenmatts*. Eds. Gerhard P. Knapp and Gerd Lambroisse. Bern: Peter Lang, 1981, 61-81.

Tiusanen, Timo. *Dürrenmatt: A Study in Plays, Prose, Theory*. Princeton: Princeton University Press, 1977.

Wright, A. M. "Scientific Method and Rationality in Dürrenmatt." *German Life and Letters* NS 35 (1981): 64-72.

Rolf Hochhuth

Durzak, Manfred. "Amerikanische Mythologien. Zu Hochhuths Dramen '*Guerillas*' und '*Tod eines Jägers*.'" *Rolf Hochhuth — Eingriff in die Zeitgeschichte: Essays zum Werk*. Ed. Walter Hinck. Reinbek: Rowohlt, 1981, 159-86.

——. "Ein Trauerspiel des Dramatikers Rolf Hochhuth. Anmerkungen zu seinem 'Judith'-Stück." *Hebbel Jahrbuch 1987*. Eds. Barbara Wellhausen, Wolfgang Damms, and Heinz Stolte. Heide: Westholsteinische Verlagsanstalt, 1987, 13-26.

Hinderer, Walter. "Hochhuth und Schiller — oder: Die Rettung des Menschen." *Rolf Hochhuth — Eingriff in die Zeitgeschichte: Essays zum Werk*. Ed. Walter Hinck. Reinbek: Rowohlt, 1981, 59-78.

Raddatz, Fritz J., "Der utopische Pessimist." *Rolf Hochhuth — Eingriff in die Zeitgeschichte: Essays zum Werk*. Ed. Walter Hinck. Reinbek: Rowohlt, 1981, 33-54.

Taeni, Rainer. *Rolf Hochhuth*. Autorenbücher 5. Munich: Beck, 1977.

Ward, Margaret. *Rolf Hochhuth*. Twayne's World Authors Series 463. Boston: Twayne, 1977.

Christoph Ransmayr

Bartsch, Kurt. "Dialog mit Antike und Mythos. Christoph Ransmayrs Ovid-Roman *Die letzte Welt*." *Modern Austrian Literature* 23.3-4 (1990): 121-33.

Cohen, Roger. "Author Updates Ovid Impertinently." *New York Times* 10 May 1990.

Hage, Volker. "Mein Name sei Ovid. Ein großer Roman: Christoph Ransmayrs *Die letzte Welt*." *Die Zeit* 7 Oct. 1988.

Nethersole, Reingard. "Marginal Topologies. Space in Christoph Ransmayr's *Die Schrecken des Eises und der Finsternis.*" *Modern Austrian Literature* 23.3-4 (1990): 135-53.

Schirrmacher, Frank. "Bücher aus Asche, Leiber aus Ameisen. Endlich ein neues Talent: Christoph Ransmayr und sein sprachgewaltiger Einbildungsroman *Die letzte Welt.*" *Frankfurter Allgemeine Zeitung* 17 Sept. 1988.

Wieser, Harald. "Eine Flaschenpost aus der Antike." *Der Spiegel* 42 (12 Sept. 1988): 226-37.

Gerhard Roth

Adrian, Sylvia. "Ich will ein Erzähler sein." *Frankfurter Hefte* Feb. 1981: 67-8.

Bauschinger, Sigrid. "Gerhard Roth." *Major Figures of Contemporary Austrian Literature.* Ed. Donald G. Daviau. New York, Berne: Peter Lang, 1987, 337-62.

Blöcker, Günter. "Ein kündiger Protokollant seelischer Irritationen. Gerhard Roths Roman *Der stille Ozean.*" *Frankfurter Allgemeine* 22 March 1980.

Grond, Walter. "Gerhard Roths *Landläufiger Tod.* Zur Genese eines Romans." *manuskripte: Zeitschrift für Literatur* 29.105 (1989): 83-91.

Hinck, Walter. "Die aus den Fugen geratene Welt des Dorfes. *Landläufiger Tod* — Gerhard Roths Roman und seine *Chronik.*" *Frankfurter Allgemeine Zeitung* 20 Nov. 1984.

Laemmle, Peter. "Die Suche nach der verlorenen Universalität. Gedanken zu Gerhard Roths epischem Großversuch *Landläufiger Tod.*" *Süddeutsche Zeitung* 23 Feb. 1985.

——. "Eintreten in die eigene Besessenheit. Gerhard Roths Prosaband *Der Untersuchungsrichter.*" *Süddeutsche Zeitung* 17 Sept. 1988.

Philippi, Klaus-Peter. "Das Leben ist der kurze Moment des Sturzes. Neue Wahrnehmungsprosa von Gerhard Roth: Ein Untersuchungsrichter zwischen Lüge und Gewalt." *Rheinischer Merkur/Christ und Welt* 25 March 1988.

Pichler, Georg. "Der Gimpel pfeift im Pfirsichgeblüh. Gerhard Roths *Untersuchungsrichter.*" *Die Presse* (Vienna) 4/5 June 1988.

Raddatz, Fritz J. "Epische Geisterbahn. Gerhard Roths *Landläufiger Tod* und *Dorfchronik* zu diesem Buch." *Die Zeit* 9 Nov. 1984.

Sebald, W. G. "In einer wildfremden Gegend. Zu Gerhard Roths Roman *Landläufiger Tod.*" *manuskripte: Zeitschrift für Literatur* 26.92 (1986): 52-56.

Peter Sloterdijk

Krättli, Anton. "Transplantationen der Vergangenheit. *Der Zauberbaum.* Zu einem epischen Versuch von Peter Sloterdijk." *Schweizer Monatshefte* 65 (1985): 427-32.

Laermann, Klaus. "Von der Apo zur Apokalypse. Resignation und Fröhliche Wissenschaft am Beispiel von Peter Sloterdijk." *"Postmoderne" oder Der Kampf um die Zukunft: Die Kontroverse in Wissenschaft, Kunst und Gesellschaft.* Ed. Peter Kemper. Frankfurt: Fischer, 1988, 207-30.

Lucht, Frank Helmut, and Albert von Schirnding, "Sloterdijks 'Kritik.' Eine Doppelkritik." *Merkur* 37 (1983): 823-31.

Merkel, Reinhard. "Imperiale Gebärde, rasante Gedanken." *Der Spiegel* 37 (13. June 1983): 172-79.

Wilson, Neil. "Punching Out the Enlightenment: A Discussion of Peter Sloterdijk's *Kritik der zynsichen Vernunft.*" *New German Critique* 41 (1987): 53-70.

Other Sources

Arbib, Michael A., and Mary B. Hesse. *The Construction of Reality* Cambridge: Cambridge University Press, 1986.

Anti-Foundationalism and Practical Reasoning: Conversations between Hermeneutics and Analysis. Ed. Evan Simpson. Edmonton: Academic Printing and Publishing, 1987.

Apel, Karl-Otto. "Is the Ethics of the Ideal Communication Community a Utopia? On the Relationship between Ethics, Utopia, and the Critique of Utopia." Trans. David Frisby. *The Communicative Ethics Controversy.* Eds. Seyla Benhabib and Fred Dallmayr. Cambridge: MIT Press, 1990, 23-59.

Aronowitz, Stanley. *Science as Power: Discourse and Ideology in Modern Society.* Minneapolis: University of Minnesota Press, 1988.

Bell, Daniel. *The Cultural Contradictions of Capitalism.* New York: Basic Books, 1976.

——. "Modernism and Capitalism." *Partisan Review* 45 (1978): 206-22.

Benhabib, Seyla. "The West German Peace Movement and Its Critics." *Telos* 51 (spring 1982): 148-58.

Berger, Peter. "Identity as a Problem in the Sociology of Knowledge." *The Sociology of Knowledge.* Eds. James E. Curtis and John W. Petras. New York: Praeger, 1970, 373-84.

——. "On the Obsolescence of the Concept of Honour." *Liberalism and Its Critics.* Ed. Michael J. Sandel. New York: New York University Press, 1984, 149-58.

——, and Thomas Luckmann. *The Social Construction of Reality: A Treatise in the Sociology of Knowledge.* Garden City, New York: Doubleday, 1966.

Berlin, Isaiah. "Two Concepts of Liberty." *Liberalism and Its Critics.* Ed. Michael J. Sandel. New York: New York University Press, 1984, 15-36.

Berman, Russell. "Opposition to Rearmament and West German Culture." *Telos* 51 (spring 1982): 141-48.

Bono, James J. "Science, Discourse, and Literature: The Role/Rule of Metaphor in Science." *Literature and Science: Theory and Practice.* Ed. Stuart Peterfreund. Boston: Northeastern University Press, 1990, 59-89.

Booth, Wayne. *Modern Dogma and the Rhetoric of Assent.* University of Notre Dame Ward-Phillips Lectures in English Language and Literature 5. Notre Dame: Notre Dame University Press; Chicago: University of Chicago Press, 1974.

Construction and Constraint: The Shaping of Scientific Rationality. Ed. Ernan McMullin. Notre Dame: Notre Dame University Press, 1988.

Dahrendorf, Ralf. *Society and Democracy in Germany.* 1967. New York: Norton, 1979.

Darnton, Robert. *Mesmerism and the End of the Enlightenment in France.* Cambridge: Harvard University Press, 1968.

Davenport, Edward. "The Devils of Positivism." *Literature and Science: Theory and Practice.* Ed. Stuart Peterfreund. Boston: Northeastern University Press, 1990, 17-31.

Dewey, John. "Creative Democracy — The Task Before Us." *The Later Works.* 17 vols. Ed. Jo Ann Boydston. Carbondale, Illinois: Southern Illinois University Press, 1988, 14: 224-30.

Eddington, Arthur. *The Philosophy of Physical Science.* Cambridge: Cambridge University Press; New York: Macmillan, 1939.

Einstein, Albert. "Geometrie und Erfahrung." *Mein Weltbild.* Ed. Carl Seelig. Berlin: Ullstein, 1989, 119-27.

Evolutionary Epistemology, Rationality, and the Sociology of Knowledge. Eds. Gerard Radnitzky and W. W. Bartley, III. La Salle: Open Court, 1987.

Feyerabend, Paul. *Against Method: Outline of an Anarchistic Theory of Knowledge.* London: NLB, 1975.

——. *Farewell to Reason.* London: Verso, 1987.

Foster, Hal. "Postmodernism: A Preface." *The Anti-Aesthetic: Essays on Postmodern Culture.* Ed. Hal Foster. Seattle: Bay Press, 1983, ix-xvi.

Foucault, Michel. *Discipline and Punish: The Birth of the Prison.* Trans. Alan Sheridan. New York: Pantheon, 1977.

——. *The Order of Things: An Archaeology of the Human Sciences.* 1966. New York: Random House, 1970.

——. "What is Enlightenment?" Trans. Catherine Porter. *The Foucault Reader.* Ed. Paul Rabinow. New York: Pantheon, 1984, 32-50.

Freud, Sigmund. *Civilization and Its Discontents.* Trans. James Strachey. New York: Norton, 1961.

Gadamer, Hans-Georg. *Reason in the Age of Science.* Trans. Frederick G. Lawrence. Cambridge: MIT Press, 1981.

Gardiner, Patrick. "German Philosophy and the Rise of Relativism." *The Monist* 64 (1981): 138-54.

van Gennep, Arnold. *The Rites of Passage*. Trans. Monika B. Vizedom and Gabrielle L. Caffee. London: Routledge and Keegan Paul, 1909.

Graff, Gerald. *Literature against Itself: Literary Ideas in Modern Society*. Chicago: University of Chicago Press, 1979.

Habermas, Jürgen. "An Alternative Way out of the Philosophy of the Subject: Communicative versus Subject-Centered Reason." *The Philosophical Discourse of Modernity*. Trans. Frederick Lawrence. Cambridge: MIT Press, 1987, 294-326.

——. "Discourse Ethics: Notes on a Program of Philosophical Justification." Trans. Shierry Weber Nicholsen and Christian Lenhardt. *The Communicative Ethics Controversy*. Eds. Seyla Benhabib and Fred Dallmayr. Cambridge: MIT Press, 1990, 60-110.

——. "Dogmatism, Reason, and Decision: On Theory and Praxis in Our Scientific Civilization." *Theory and Practice*. Trans. John Viertel. Boston: Beacon Press, 1973, 253-82.

——. "Die Einheit der Vernunft in der Vielheit ihrer Stimmen." *Merkur* 42 (1988): 1-14.

——. *Knowledge and Human Interests*. Trans. Jeremy J. Shapiro. Boston: Beacon Press, 1971.

——. "Modernity versus Postmodernity." Trans. Seyla Benhabib. *New German Critique* 22 (1981): 3-14.

——. "New Social Movements." *Telos* 49 (fall 1981): 32-37.

——. "A Philosophico-Political Profile." *New Left Review* 151 (May/June 1985): 71-105.

——. "A Positivistically Bisected Rationalism." *The Positivist Dispute in German Sociology*. Trans. Glyn Adey and David Frisby. London: Heinemann, 1976, 198-225.

——. "The Public Sphere: An Encyclopedia Article (1964)." Trans. Sara Lennox and Frank Lennox. *New German Critique* 1.3 (1974): 49-55. Originally published in *Fischer Lexikon: Staat und Politik*. Frankfurt: Fischer, 1964, 220-26.

——. *Reason and the Rationalization of Society*. Vol. 1 of *The Theory of Communicative Action*. Trans. Thomas McCarthy. Boston: Beacon Press, 1984.

——. "The Scientization of Politics and Public Opinion." *Towards a Rational Society: Student Protest, Science, and Politics*. Trans. Jeremy Shapiro. Boston: Beacon Press, 1970, 62-80.

——. *Structural Transformation of the Public Sphere: An Inquiry into a Category of Bourgeois Society*. Trans. Thomas Burger and Frederick Lawrence. 1962. Cambridge: MIT Press, 1989.

Harvey, David. *The Condition of Postmodernity: An Inquiry into the Origins of Cultural Change*. London: Basil Blackwell, 1989.

Heidegger, Martin. *Basic Writings*. Ed. David Farrell Krell. New York: Harper and Row, 1977.

Hirsch, Joachim. "The West German Peace Movement." Trans. David Berger. *Telos* 51 (spring 1982): 135-41.

Hohendahl, Peter. "Critical Theory, Public Sphere, and Culture: Jürgen Habermas and His Critics." Trans. Marc Silverman. *The Institution of Criticism*. Ithaca: Cornell University Press, 1982, 242-80.

Honneth, Axel. "Foucault und Adorno. Zwei Formen einer Kritik der Moderne." *"Postmoderne" oder der Kampf um die Zukunft: Die Kontroverse in Wissenschaft, Kunst und Gesellschaft*. Ed. Peter Kemper. Frankfurt: Fischer, 1988, 127-44.

Horkheimer, Max, and Theodor Adorno. *Dialectic of Enlightenment*. Trans. John Cumming. 1944. New York: Continuum, 1972.

Huysmans, J. K. "Preface Written Twenty Years After the Novel" [1903]. *Against the Grain (A Rebours)*. New York: Dover, 1969, xxxiii-xlix.

Iser, Wolfgang. *The Implied Reader: Patterns of Communication in Prose Fiction from Bunyan to Beckett*. Baltimore: Johns Hopkins University Press, 1974.

James, William. *Writings 1902-1910*. Ed. Bruce Kuklick. New York: Library of America, 1987.

Jameson, Frederick. "Postmodernism and Consumer Society." *The Anti-Aesthetic: Essays on Postmodern Culture*. Ed. Hal Foster. Seattle: Bay Press, 1983, 111-25.

Kant, Immanuel. Preface to the Second Edition. *Critique of Pure Reason*. Trans. F. Max Müller. Garden City, New York: Anchor, 1966, xxviii-xlvi.

Kuhn, Thomas. "Logic of Discovery or Psychology of Research." *The Essential Tension: Selected Studies in Scientific Tradition and Change*. Chicago: University of Chicago Press, 1977, 266-292.

——. *The Structure of Scientific Revolutions*. 2nd ed. International Encyclopedia of Unified Science, vol.2, no.2. Chicago: University of Chicago Press, 1970.

Laqueur, Walter. *Germany Today: A Personal Report*. Boston: Little, Brown, 1985.

Lenzen, Victor F. "Einstein's Theory of Knowledge." *Albert Einstein: Philosopher-Scientist*. Ed. Paul Arthur Schillp. 3rd ed. The Library of Living Philosophers 7. La Salle, Illinois: Open Court, 1970, 355-84.

Literature on the Threshold: The German Novel in the 1980s. Eds. Arthur Williams, Stuart Parkes, and Roland Smith. Oxford: Berg, 1990.

Livingston, Paisley. *Literary Knowledge: Humanistic Inquiry and the Philosophy of Science*. Ithaca: Cornell University Press, 1988.

Lyotard, Jean-François. *The Postmodern Condition: A Report on Knowledge*. Trans. Geoff Bennington and Brian Massumi. Theory and History of Literature 10. Minneapolis: University of Minnesota Press, 1984.

Marcuse, Herbert. "On Science and Phenomenology." *The Essential Frankfurt School Reader*. Eds. Andrew Arato and Eike Gebhardt. New York: Continuum, 1982, 466-76.

——. *One-Dimensional Man: Studies in the Ideology of Advanced Industrial Society*. Boston: Beacon Press, 1964.

Margolis, Joseph. *Pragmatism without Foundations: Reconciling Realism and Relativism*. Oxford: Basil Blackwell, 1986.

McCarthy, Thomas. *The Critical Theory of Jürgen Habermas*. Cambridge: MIT Press, 1978.

McGowan, John. *Postmodernism and Its Critics*. Ithaca: Cornell University Press, 1991.

McHale, Brian. *Postmodernist Fiction*. New York: Methuen, 1987.

McLellan, David. *Ideology*. Minneapolis: University of Minnesota Press, 1986.

Nägele, Rainer. "Modernism and Postmodernism: The Margins of Articulation." *Studies in Twentieth Century Literature* 5 (1980): 5-25.

Popper, Karl R. *Conjectures and Refutations: The Growth of Scientific Knowledge*. 1962. New York: Harper, 1965.

———. *The Logic of Scientific Discovery*. 1934. New York: Basic Books, 1959.

———. "The Myth of the Framework." *The Abdication of Philosophy: Philosophy and the Public Good*. Ed. Eugene Freeman. LaSalle: Open Court, 1976, 23-48.

———. "Normal Science and Its Dangers." *Criticism and the Growth of Knowledge*. Eds. Imre Lakatos and Alan Musgrave. Proceedings of the International Colloquium in the Philosophy of Science, London, 1965, vol. 4. Cambridge: Cambridge University Press, 1970, 51-58.

———. *Objective Knowledge: An Evolutionary Approach*. Oxford: Clarendon Press, 1972.

———. *The Open Society and Its Enemies*. 5th ed. 2 vols. Princeton: Princeton University Press, 1966.

———. *Popper: Selections*. Ed. David Miller. Princeton: Princeton University Press, 1985.

———. *The Poverty of Historicism*. 3rd ed. 1961. New York: Harper, 1964.

The Positivist Dispute in German Sociology. Trans. Glyn Adey and David Frisby. London: Heinemann, 1976.

Pusey, Michael. *Jürgen Habermas*. Chichester, England: Ellis Horwood, 1987.

Raskin, Marcus G., and Herbert J. Bernstein. *New Ways of Knowing: The Sciences, Society, and Reconstructive Knowledge*. Totowa, New Jersey: Rowman and Littlefield, 1987.

Relativism: Cognitive and Moral. Eds. Jack W. Meiland and Michael Krausz. Notre Dame: Notre Dame University Press, 1982.

Rorty, Richard. *Consequences of Pragmatism. Essays: 1972-1980*. Minneapolis: University of Minnesota Press, 1982.

———. *Contingency, Irony, Solidarity*. Cambridge: Cambridge University Press, 1989.

———. "Habermas and Lyotard on Postmodernity." *Habermas and Modernity*. Ed. Richard J. Bernstein. Cambridge: MIT Press, 1985, 161-75.

———. *Philosophy and the Mirror of Nature*. Princeton: Princeton University Press, 1979.

———. "Science as Solidarity." *The Rhetoric of the Human Sciences: Language and Argument in Scholarship and Public Affairs*. Eds. John S. Nelson, Allan Megill, and Donald N. McCloskey. Madison: University of Wisconsin Press, 1987, 38-52.

———. "Soldarity or Objectivity?" *Relativism: Interpretation and Confrontation*. Ed. Michael Krausz. Notre Dame: Notre Dame University Press, 1989, 35-50.

Russell, Bertrand. "Philosophy and Politics." *Unpopular Essays*. New York: Simon and Schuster, 1950, 1-20.

Singer, Peter. "On Being Silenced in Germany." *New York Review of Books* 15 August 1991: 36-42.

Smart, Barry. *Michel Foucault*. Chichester, England: Ellis Horwood, 1985.

Taylor, Charles. "From Marxism to the Dialogue Society." *From Culture to Revolution: The Slant Symposium 1967*. Eds. Terry Eagleton and Brian Wicker. London: Sheed and Ward, 1968, 148-81.

Toulmin, Stephen. *Cosmopolis: The Hidden Agenda of Modernity*. New York: The Free Press, 1990.

Turner, Victor. "Liminal to Liminoid, in Play, Flow, and Ritual: An Essay in Comparative Symbology." *Rice University Studies* 60.3 (1974): 53-92.

——. *The Ritual Process: Structure and Anti-Structure*. 1969. Ithaca: Cornell University Press, 1977.

Vaihinger, Hans. *The Philosophy of "As If": A System of the Theoretical, Practical and Religious Fictions of Mankind*. Trans. C. K. Ogden. 2nd ed. London: Routledge and Keegan Paul, 1935.

Weber, Max. "Science as a Vocation." *From Max Weber: Essays in Sociology*. Trans. H. H. Gerth and C. Wright Mills. Oxford: Oxford University Press, 1946, 129-156.

White, Stephen K. *The Recent Work of Jürgen Habermas: Reason, Justice and Morality*. Cambridge: Cambridge University Press, 1988.

Wittenberg, Alexander Israel. *Vom Denken in Begriffen: Mathematik als Experiment des reinen Denkens*. Basel: Birkhäuser, 1957.

Wittgenstein, Ludwig. *Tractatus Logico-Philosophicus*. Trans. D. F. Pears and B. F. McGuinness. London: Routledge and Kegan Paul, 1961.

Wood, Allen W. "Habermas' Defense of Rationalism." *New German Critique* 35 (1985): 145-64.

Index